1. Introduction to course of lectures and notes
   a. Your options what to learn and how, scale of business
   b. How much stuff can you sell on amazon.com and eBay
   c. How big is amazon.com and ebay.com are, potential
   d. Topics that we will discuss
   e. Establish players in the process
   f. Possibilities for your business
   g. Your product line assessment
   h. Perception of your business online
   i.
2. Security
   a. Ownership
   b. Fraud
   c. Segregation
   d. Unique
3. Shipping
   a. Returns
   b. Packaging
   c. Slip
   d. Protecting from water
4. Listing
   a. Description
   b. Image (resolution, size, quality, background, studio, light, proportions, number of images, additional images)
   c. Where to get isbn
   d. Bar code
   e. Other unique numbers
5. Reviews
   a. Written review
   b. College kids review
   c. Neighbors reviews
   d. Family members review
   e. Facebook.com and off line friends reviews
   f. Video reviews
   g. Key words for review
   h. How to start and close your review
   i. Different words have to be in each review
   j. Amazon does not allow to pay for reviews
   k.
6. Feedback
7. Useful tips
8. Brand building
9. Amazon EBay regulations
10. Customer Service
    a. Keeping templates of your common letters for re use

        b. Sending responses on time
11. Supporting documents
        a. Business plan template
        b. Model release form
12. Frequently asking questions FAQ
13. Reviews
14. Feedback
15. Useful tips
16. Brand building
17. Amazon EBay regulations
18. Customer Service
19. Supporting documents
20. How to Build up the account?
21. How to Protect account from Competition?
22. How to control many accounts?
23. How to sell more?
24. How to take better pictures?
25. How to write a description?

Dedications for the Amazon and EBay notes by Alexander Gurman 2014

To my son Gary Gurman, my inspiration, my muse "baby needs new shoes". I intent to make money selling this book and selling on Amazon and EBay thanks to my book myself and I want everybody who would read this book to be able to make money.

I am grateful to my wife Lana Holovko for her love and ability to proof read my drafts. For her understanding that time spend in writing this book has been lost as quality family time with Lana.
Thank you Dasha Romer for your grammar corrections, thank you for helping me to package gift items, thank you for reviews and for the photography advice.

I am grateful first and foremost to Oleg Atlasman for his guidance to my path of seller on EBay and Amazon, thanks to Oleg I know waist majority of the information I operates based on. Many secrets and research ideals in this book have been shared by Oleg with me free of charge and this book has been born in many ways because of Oleg guidance.

Thank you my brother Gennady for his drawings and paintings for this book and for other suggestions.

Thank you to my father for his writing support and being the first who told that this book could be sold in numbers and for his encouragement to write it.
Thank you to my students Alex, Dmitry, and Alexander for there questions during writing the script.

Thank you to EBay and Amazon community for sharing ideals and suggestions what to write and what to include.
I am open to suggestions, stories and experience that from you that we can share with the world. Email me Alexander@AlexGurman.com or call 917 825 8225

Alexander Gurman has been an Amazon.com and Ebay.com seller for many years and sells in variety of product lines. Alexander sells his father Efroim Gurman book on grooming www.TheGroomingBook.com A Comprehensive Manual for Individualized Dog and Cat Grooming.
Alexander makes and sells fishing tackle Gurmana Korablik at ebay.com and amazon.com www.BargeFishing.com
Alexander sells fishing bait glue that he makes at Amazon.com and Ebay.com www.FishingBaitGlue.com
Alexander owns Amazon and EBay distribution rights for product line from Vet Vitttles inc www.VetVittles.com
Alexander writes books on subjects of fishing and hunting and sell them at Amazon and EBay.
Alexander holds distribution rights for the Mur Mur Fashion swimwear in the North America www.MurMurFashion.com

Alexander Gurman holds degree in Marketing Management from Baruch College in NYC, USA. Alexander also has combine B.S. and M.S. degree in Biochemistry from Odessa State University.

Combination of the product lines above and writing experience and publishing experience with his father books position Alexander in unique spot to give advice to new and experience Amazon and EBay sellers.

Alexander is an avid photographer and videographer and that also helps in on line sales Alexander have spend his first 7 years in the USA as computer programmer and web designer.
Professionally Alexander on his day job gives financial advice for a fee at the bank.

Alexander gives private lessons on Amazon and EBay selling in Brooklyn NY, and over skype alexandergurman You can contact Alexander directly at 917 825 8225 or email Alexander@AlexGurman.com

1. **Introduction to course of lectures and notes**
    a. **Your options what to learn and how, scale of business**

You can be as little as few item a day as hobby seller.

You can use this book just to clear space in your garage to sell unwanted items

You can become Titanium power seller with 3 to 6 million dollar monthly sales

Limits are endless here

You may know more than I do about selling or you may find few useful ideas, I think it still worth it even if you find one useful idea for you to save yourself from negative feedback, or save account from closing for stupid mistake or to increase your sales much more than what is the cost of this book.

    b. **How much stuff can you sell on amazon.com and eBay**

You can start small and grow fast to 5-6 thousand dollars in sales within few months to a year. I have a friend right now who does what I advice him to do and he makes 1,6 million in annual sales.

    c. **How big is amazon.com and ebay.com are, potential**
    d. **How big is amazon.com?**

Traded as NASDAQ: AMZN price **285.73** NASDAQ-100 Component S&P 500 Component Foundation date 1994 Headquarters Seattle, Washington, United States Area served Worldwide Founder Jeff Bezos Key people Jeff Bezos Chairman, President & CEO Industry Internet, online retailing Products A2Z Development, A9.com, Alexa Internet, Amazon.com, Amazon Kindle, Amazon Studios, Amazon Web Services, Audible.com, dpreview.com, Endless.com, IMDb, LoveFilm, The Book Depository, Zappos.com, Woot, Junglee.com, goodreads.com, myhabit.com, askville Revenue US$ 61.09 billion Operating income US$ 0676 million Net income US$ 0−39 million Total assets US$ 32.55 billion Total equity US$ 08.19 billion Employees 91,300 Amazon.com various national sites Written in C++, Perl and Java Type of site E-commerce Advertising Web banners, videos Available in English, French, German, Spanish, Italian, Japanese, Chinese, Brazilian Portuguese Launched 1995

How big is ebay.com
The eBay Public Traded as NASDAQ: EBAY price now is 54.00 NASDAQ-100 Component S&P 500 Component Foundation date September 3, 1995 Headquarters San Jose, California, U.S. Area served Worldwide Founder(s) Pierre Omidyar Key people Pierre Omidyar Chairman John Donahoe CEO Industry Internet, Online retailing Products eBayClassifieds, electronic commerce, Gumtree, Kijiji, online auction hosting, PayPal, iBazar Revenue US$ 14.07 billion Operating income US$ 02.88 billion Net income US$ 02.60 billion Total assets US$ 37.27 billion Total equity US$ 20.87 billion Employees 27,770 Slogan(s) "World's Online Marketplace." "Connecting buyers and sellers

globally." "Whatever it is, you can get it on eBay." "Buy it, sell it, love it" "Buy it New, Buy it Now" "When it's on your mind, it's on eBay" eBay.com written in Java, Python IPv6 support No Type of site Online auction Registration Required to buy and sell Available in Multilingual Key Statistics Get Key Statistics for: Market Cap (intraday)5: 69.63B Enterprise Value (Jul 5, 2013)3: 62.24B Trailing P/E (ttm, intraday): 26.05 Forward P/E (fye Dec 31, 2014)1: 16.62 PEG Ratio (5 yr expected)1: 1.28 Price/Sales (ttm): 4.74 Price/Book (mrq): 3.26 Enterprise Value/Revenue (ttm)3: 4.28 Enterprise Value/EBITDA (ttm)6: 14.44 Profitability Profit Margin (ttm): 18.68% Operating Margin (ttm): 21.06% Management Effectiveness Return on Assets (ttm): 5.78% Return on Equity (ttm): 13.64% Income Statement Revenue (ttm): 14.54B Revenue Per Share (ttm): 11.24 Qtrly Revenue Growth (yoy): 14.40% Gross Profit (ttm): 9.86B EBITDA (ttm)6: 4.31B Net Income Avl to Common (ttm): 2.72B Diluted EPS (ttm): 2.06 Qtrly Earnings Growth (yoy): 18.80% Balance Sheet Total Cash (mrq): 9.40B Total Cash Per Share (mrq): 7.25 Total Debt (mrq): 4.52B Total Debt/Equity (mrq): 21.39 Current Ratio (mrq): 1.91 Book Value Per Share (mrq): 16.30 Cash Flow Statement Operating Cash Flow (ttm): 4.24B Levered Free Cash Flow (ttm): 1.48B

Alibaba.com

Chinese e-commerce giant Alibaba sold one trillion RMB worth of goods in 2012, the company announced today. That's $157 billion U.S. in gross merchandise volume (GMV), which easily surpasses U.S e-commerce giants Amazon and eBay combined.

In fact, Alibaba chairman Jack Ma said only two companies have ever recorded annual transaction volumes at this level: Wal-Mart and Alibaba.

Alibaba — which recorded $3 billion in sales in a single day earlier this year — is a conglomerate primarily composed of Tmall, which manages e-commerce operations for thousands of companies in China, and Taobao Marketplace, a rough equivalent of eBay. All payments are handled by Alipay, the company's own payments processor, and Alipay has over 700 million registered users — with credit card information.

The company has grown massively in the past four years as the Chinese middle class increases in size and wealth, and as it has become a hub for a massive share of Chinese e-commerce. E-commerce has been growing at 60 percent year-over-year in 2012 in China's third and fourth-tier cities, the company says, and currently just over five percent of all Chinese retail spending – RMB 18.39 trillion — passes through Alibaba websites.

And it's not looking backward, as chairman and CEO Jack Ma made clear: "It's very likely that next year our transaction volume will be bigger than all the American e-commerce companies combined," Ma said in a company statement. In 2012 so far, the company has accounted for an amazing 60 percent of all packages delivered in China — an astounding 12 million packages a day. That's up from an average of eight million packages a day in 2011.

The company measures GMV, a sales equivalent that takes into account all product sold by clients who use Alibaba's e-commerce infrastructure to enable their own sales, and all Chinese consumers or businesses that sell their products on Taobao's marketplace. The measure is roughly equivalent to gross sales, but an important distinction is that most of the profits of each sale do not reside with Alibaba, which takes a small percentage. That's not entirely dissimilar to Amazon, which facilitates the sale of many other companies' products, or eBay, which takes a small percentage of any item you might sell on the site.

Alibaba is predicting three trillion RMB of total volume of sales through its various sites in 2017, which would be $471 billion, and would surpass Wal-Mart's current sales of about $444 billion.

Amazon's annual sales volumes are in the $50-60 billion range, with quarterly sales of $13 to $15 billion. eBay sold about $5 billion 2011 and is projecting about $8 billion in sales in 2012. The U.S e-commerce market, however, is much more fractured than the Chinese market, with many companies taking small slices of the overall pie.

Yahoo still owns a stake in Alibaba — about 23 percent after selling half of its shares for $7.6 billion earlier this year.

e. Topics that we will discuss
Where to buy products,
How to sell them,
How to protect your account,
How to grow your business
What to do so your business would grow and you would sell more than competitors.

f. Establish players in the process
We will establish who works with account,
Who does market research?
Who does sales?
Who does listing, imaging, and customer service?

g. Possibilities for your business
Large, small, slow or fast moving, how much can you invest in the business now.

h. Your product line assessment
What do you sell, why do you sell that product,
How much diversify are you,
What would you do if you can not sell that product for whatever reason?
What is your back up plan?

i. Perception of your business online

How do you perceive your business online?

Shipping for EBay and Amazon notes by Alexander Gurman 2014

1. **How to ship items?** Actually print the label from your printer and glue label to the package and take it the post office. I use by now self gluing paper that shared in two labels, that is convenient and great saving in time. Ship on time, ship proper products, ship proper amount of products in each package, if someone ordered two items make a note for yourself that is two items and check. Do not mismatch packaging slips and shipping labels. You can print all slips and all labels and than pack. Or you can print one label and one package slip and pack and move the next, if you do small amounts that is fine, in large quantities try to do one thing at a time. Keep cameras recording process of packaging especially if someone else is doing it and even if you do it. You can store that quite cheap on your dropbox spaces, and that way in case theft will show up you can see where the loss took place, it also show some prove for the EBay and Amazon and for your buyers that you actually dedicated to detail process and misstate most likely may happen in other places, but not in your assembly line.

2. **Free shipping** domestic
Since our customers are well spoiled, free shipping is a great way to attract more customers to your listing, you can include shipping cost in your calculations of the expenses but than people have a feeling that they get something for free and go for product more than competitor's products. The problem here is that customers who wants everything free are also yours, they get the product and than send you email, if they can get their money back for whatever reason, because they know that your feedback is important for you and you may agree to gift them your product, only not to receive negative feedback that can kill your sales. Be careful, beware of what you wish for, it may happen in the worth possible scenario.

3. **International shipping**

4. **Shipping policies**
Establish your shipping policy, try to ship the same day, explain that you have few computers, few printers, extra packaging supply, extra ink for your printer, power battery for your computers, extra help when you on vacations, that way you can insure your buyers that you are reliable shipping partner. Explain your policy in detail; make it in bullet points easy to read.

5. **Same day shipping:** try to offer and do same day shipping, people loves to receive goods right away and speed is very important in online sales. You will have more sales and good feedback based on speed.

6. **Package slip**: do not forget to include it, it is the law. Try to customize slip, include your business card, if you like the buyer and expect more

sales to the same buyer try to include affordable gift. Personal notes also go a long way.

7. **Packaging:** package so it will have water protection, put extra bubbles, if it can break use good boxes. Do not carry products that can get heat damage in your car for a long time without AC. Protect your products. When you leave your product at the post office window make sure that it not get stolen by the next person, close window. If you have time give packages to post office clerk directly, as to scan it and give you receipts. Use good quality printer and good ink to print labels, that way you will make sure that it will be screamed by computer for tracking purposes, it will put some calm in the eyes of your buyers to watch their item while arriving to them.

8. **Video of the packaging:** if you sending expensive items, video tape packaging of the product and store it for a while, in case you will have a dispute it may help you with amazon.com or ebay.com representative to prove that you actually put the right item in the package.

9. **Invisible ink** on signs: you can buy pen with invisible ink and sign your products with it, and also video record this activity and talk about it in your policies. That can scare scammers and give you more credibility that your products are authentic and you have been around and know how to protect your rights. Those fraud scammers who read your disclaimer may decide to avoid starting a fight with you and you will save yourself some aggravation.

10. **Storing products,**
Store products organized, know where do you store and what. I store in boxes and on top of each box I put a page with short inventory of what I have in that box. I try to store in transparent boxes to see what I have in each box without opening each one. I also like boxes with cover and that protected from flood and heat in the attic.
Have extra packaging tape, bubbles, and ink always save. Know your way to staple.com in case of need but staples.com does not have the best prices, best prices are online. So buy in advance.

11. **Where to buy bubbles:** I think right now best prices are on ebay.com or look for big suppliers, perhaps you can buy first time on ebay.com and than you can buy from the same supplier directly and save on ebay.com fee. Sometimes I locate suppliers on ebay.com initially and than find them online and negotiate prices directly. Sometimes I prefer to buy on ebay.com because than I have guaranteed to be able to return items, when I buy directly I have no control such as paypal.com services.

12. **Water protection** for your products and packages. Keep your boxes in dry location so boxes will not get moist, then they would weight more and post office will change you more and some of your shipments can come back to you for luck of weight. Also try protecting product from moist, over time products will smell in bad vented places. Have clear air.

13. **Wracking shipping,** too heavy tape is not good because it extra weight, too light, you risk that your package will break. I like 3m and buy it on liquidation.com I also recommend to have good tape dispenser and perhaps one extra spear one dispenser. They tent to get lost in the right moment; also you might need extra one for help if you service the account with your spouse or partner at the same time.

14. **Proper weight**
When I list items proper weight is important even when I offer free shipping on domestic products, because in case you sell something internationally and you can go broke if you put wrong weight, in many occasions ebay.com and amazon.com will pay you less than that international post office would charge big time and it will kill the sense to do business, so I put some more weight a bit, just in case. Also you need to calculate the weight of the package and bubbles, it all add up to item weight in scale.

15. **Proper dimensions:** will affect your shipping rates, too much you enter and you paying extra, not enough enter and you risk that item will get returned to you and you end up with un happy customer who was waiting for the item and did not get it.

16. **Proper packaging:** do not be lazy and cheap, package in new bubbles, do not use old bubbles that have been in use that would make your package look new and fresh, I even use female colon to spray my items so they smell nice when they will arrive. Guys love that.

17. **Your shipping policies** if you have clear answer that you do not return money after lets say 60 days and someone wants to return, you can do almost nothing about it, that will prevent receiving complaint or negative feedback but still good shipping policy will help. Read some of your competitors policies, read policies of the best sellers on ebay.com and amazon.com write for yourself something appropriate. I will include here my policy as an example what you can do for you.

18. **UPS** – great shipping company for the heavy stuff, I like it because every staples has one drop office and staples are open early as 8 am and close as late 10 pm, obviously know the schedule of your local staples and they will also give you receipt that you ship so many boxes. For amazon.com UPS is your natural choice since it is preferred amazon.com partner right now.

19. **USPS**- would be the most cheap shipping method for basic needs that you may have. Some offices are open on Saturdays, some offices are open until 5 pm, know your local offices schedule, allow dropping in the window. Be careful, a lot of stealing is going on by the competitors. Try to ask postman/ post woman to put your stuff away. Use special bags so your stuff does not commingle with there people boxes, that way it is more difficult to steal from you in the drop ship window. Again if you ship in bulk you can open account with them and negotiate better rates. Some services have free envelops and free boxes, Research carefully what service do you prefer and why, some times flat rate box makes sense some times not. Figure it out for your specific need if it makes sense.

20. **FEDEX** – great to send documents, there are countries where it makes sense to use FEDEX, open account if that is what you like and you can get a discount

21. **DHL**- mostly for Europe, that is great service, very expensive, but if you sell expensive watches, or jewelry that should be your preferred choice with insurance of course.

22. **EMS** – works great for the china, most preferred choice to receive items from aliexpress.com, like every other service has tracking packages system.

23. **MIST Ukraine** – probably the cheapest and most reliable among carries who promise to deliver to Ukraine. Once a month from NYC they send container, know the day so you do not have to wait for the next month day later.

24. **Uzbekistan air** – there are few right now who offer service, I like the one that is by 86 street, I think they are more reliable and have good relationships with duty officers in Uzbekistan, which is important that expensive items would not get stolen and duties would not be 10 times the cost of the products.

25. **Duties**
When you ship internationally you have a choice to answer is that a gift of merchandise. If you check it is merchandise than buyer will have to pay duties some times, quite hefty. So many buyers ask to check it as gift and very upset if you do not put it as gift. The problem that if you follow that path you are committing custom duties fraud and same customer can turn on you and write to ebay.com or amazon.com that you did a fraud even that they and only they benefit from it. That is something that would bring you in violation with policy. Do not go in that path. Try to stay legal, you do not want for someone lose your account and right to sell on ebay.com and amazon.com for ever.

26. **Free shipping**

Is a great way to attract business mostly I do that for the USA local sales, I would say even exclusively for the USA market. That feature puts you in better search position on ebay.com site

27. **Including business cards** is a great practice, that helps to establish direct contact with buyers and in the future they can buy directly from you also gives you more legitimacy so less complains.

28. **Printers for the labels, taps, shipping labels**
Because labels are printed in bulk I would recommend for savings purpose use laser printers black and white and to refill cartridges.

29. **Gift wrapping** I always offer this option, it cost very little to have a little bit of gift wrapping materials at the shipping location, my home in my case, but I can charge a bit more and make more money with gift wrapping. Very rare used by my customers, but that is just me. It could be quite different for your case.

30. **Shipping deadlines, shipping scanning**
Both eBay and Amazon have deadline policies, now soon you have to ship and it is spelled out in your product details for each product and you can have your general policy. Try not to ship late, both eBay and Amazon will penalize you missed deadlines. Try to print on good paper with good ink in large labels because small labels even save paper can not always be read by the scanning machine and you will have no tracking information on the products. And worried customers and may loose a fight at the case center because computer at the post office could not read your scan able part of code of the shipping label.

31. **Quality of the printer ink on labels**
Have good quality ink in laser printers, ink is cheap, even if you do not do volume, will save you a lot of headache.

32. **Delivery confirmation**
Check if you want to have delivery confirmation on expensive products, so you know it was delivered.

33. **Drop shipping**
Drop shipping is when you take orders and email or somehow send orders to warehouse to mail to final customer, they just go and drop boxes at the post office. You can be located in China and ship from NYC USA whenever it product gets sold and vise versa, usually people preferred to receive items from local places and also like to place orders from local sellers, that is not always possible. But that is the wining combination.
I think customers prefer to receive orders from the USA and main civilized economies like France, Britain, Germany, Japan, Canada and Australia, products sold and shipped from other countries somehow perceived less favorable.

34. What do to when not delivered

When product is not arriving to shipped destination few things can go wrong.

    a. mail man have stolen it at the point of shipping
    b. mail man lost it at the point of shipping
    c. mail man lost it at the point of shipping
    d. your shipping employee lost if or stole it
    e. mail office lost it
    f. mail office shipped it to wrong address
    g. mail man at the point of delivery lost or stole the package
    h. neighbor stole the package
    i. customer receive the package but forgot about it
    j. customer spouse or roommate receive it and forget to mention it to customer
    k. dog eats it
    l. delivered to wrong address because buyer put one address and meant another

Solutions:

    a. send another product
    b. return money fully or partially without shipping cost, it is between you and buyer and your policy
    c. as buyer to wait a bit longer
    d. track the package online and see where it stock
    e. Verify address and confirm it upfront if you can spot once that can go wrong, good luck with that.

35. **Packaging slip and instruction how to use product**: if you sell something that require assembly or could be screw up in putting together, I would recommend include instruction how to use it to include, that would prevent you from problems as following. Let's say you sell iphone cases and include a screen for the front, and if you will not explain in your listing and not include a slip explaining how to glue cover, you may get complaint that it gets glued incorrectly by a buyer.

36. **Buying postage in bulk-** when you will start selling a lot you can negotiate rates with FEDEX, DHL and even USPS. The more you buy the better deep discount you can ask for.

37. **Deliver products in person locally** – on heavy items that is a good solution and opportunity for up sell.

38. **Pick up local sales**: that is great way to establish relationships outside of websites directly with your clients and save on shipment. Perhaps next order they can place with you directly.

39. **Do not ship to other addresses that client provide** to amazon.com or ebay.com even if you asked that is against sites policies and if products gets lost or clients decide to dispute it, you will lose that case. If you asked to send to different address explain that customer has to change there address in the system and it will generate new proper address on your end as well.

Listing

1. **Where to get unique numbers:** websites like lulu.com offers free isbn numbers for the self publishing, you can name your product same way as you name your book at lulu.com and than it would be searchable anywhere online and you will have a bar code in addition to ISBN.

2. **EBay listing**
You can list new items independently or in bulk, you can list in variations. There are no little things in the listing. Grammar is important, pictures are important, your return policy and general policy is important. Title has to include all your main key words, and starts with the most important key word. Also start your listing with main key word and line and finish with it as well. That is for the search engines, they tend to read first and last line of text and rank by it.

3. **Closing accounts is final**
If your account is closed that is final decision by either amazon.com and by ebay.com they get more new people ten times more than they close accounts so that is how they try to keep sellers in line. If the account is just blocked because you have invoice to proof for your product, than even year later you can find this invoice, fax or scan and email to them and than they will unlock your account. But if account is closed that is final and all the related accounts would be closed with it. Amazon.com and ebay.com will consider as related accounts all accounts with any peace of information that match. Same email addresses, same address, same phone number, same ip address, same shipping address. If you planning to work on few accounts at once and want to protect one against the other account, make sure that accounts are totally separate and not link in anyway to each other.

4. **Violations**
You can get violation for selling products that are prohibited by website policy like medications, or firearms, or brands that do not authorize you to sell there products like Burberry and Chanel, in order to sell those brands you need to contract them on amazon.com or ebay.com and ask a permission if that is your one item, most likely they will let you. Just be careful you do not want to get violations. Violations will place you in lower rating and your products will not be so well searchable as folks who have fully comply with their policies. Each site is a bit different and they evolve by minute but that is general perception. Be compliant, if you do not know, call customer service and ask.

5. **Selling without brand permission**
Get permission on the site.

6. **Description writing**: description has to be detail, has precise measurement of the product,
7. **Duration of the listing:**

Try to list that way that listing does not end, just add more items so you have a nice ratio between sold and available for sale, try to keep it like 50 sold and 10 available for sale, the danger that you face here is that in case all ten get sold to one or few buyers before you get a chance to add more you will lose old listing and you would have to start all over again

Do not lose old listing with sales, because they are searching better.

8. Key Words
Are the words how people may find you (if you sell products for dogs you can use dog, if you sell furniture use furniture) use more common names, if you sell brand name, is the name, have size in, color,

9. Creating new products
In order to do so you can make new product, use free lulu.com isbn for unique number and list on amazon.com or ebay.com, create name, brand etc, you would need to make packaging, instruction and to become legalized in every aspect, make sure that it is legal to sell that product online and amazon.com and ebay.com allows to sell under your brand that you created. Can not use existing established brand to pretend similar because you got sued.

10. Creating new listing

11. Variations
When you creating product you have a chance to create variations in size and in color and other parameters that you choice fit. The good thing about variations that you can advertise just one product, collect likes and reviews for one product versus creating a group of products that would spread out your time and efforts, but will have many unique numbers

12. **Title of product** Is very important, look for the best possible title with all the key words in it. It has to spell easy words and words that people search by.

13. Do not copy products from others
But others might copy product, pictures from you, put watermark on your pictures, fight if you find that someone is using exact your description that you created to sell their products, you can ask them to remove there copy of your description and write theirs otherwise you can complain to Amazon and EBay. Copying is a serious offence in online super stores like that.

14. Colors in description
I like to write in simple black color that I think does not annoy customers, but if you have taste try to experiment with variety of colors, perhaps your descriptions would not be so dull and plain and may stand out. I go for simplicity and number of listings.

15. Fond Size in description

I like to use Ariel fond or Time New Roman as basic fond and size 14 or 18 are my favorites, not too small and not to large to annoy someone.
Easy to read, I think that is a good proportion.

16. Template in description
When you save your templates, save them in the following orders, pictures, instructions for the product, description, policy for the product for shipments and refunds.

17. Templates
Some templates you can create for yourself for later use. Keep them, you can buy templates but I think that is a waist of money at the beginner stage, it only makes sense when you will start selling in very large volume when every little thing means more sales drastically.

18. Copywriting
Try not to use copywriter pictures or copywriter material, in fact trade mark your work so your competitors would not be able to use your pictures.

19. Newsletter
Start a newsletter on your products and business advice, you will get some follow up that can translate into more repeat,

20. Emotional buyers and calculated buyers

21. Distortion
You can find cases when folk's distort conditions of the product or its characteristics. You can call them on the case, especially if you are the buyer in that sense. Stick to facts and details. Do not buy in those cases, that just headache for you.

22. Extortion from you
You may get fraudulent folks who would try to extort from you free product and even money for threading you with negative feedback or threats to close your account. Show the messages to EBay and Amazon immediately try to block those people explain to sites who we dealing here. You may save the account and feedback and your money.

23. Reserve

Is the minimum price that seller is willing to sell for, it makes some times to buy at that price if you really need the product and you checked and no one else selling it cheaper and you actually need that product. I tend not to put reserve because that shows my bottom line to everyone and kind of prevent me from selling products at higher prices.

24. **Word press** Great software, very popular to run social websites, not very friendly to e commerce but good for promotional reasons. Provide you with tools to control your page and feedback that you get in the blogs and from the website visitors.
25. **Listing items** in inches and cm and in kg and pounds because you do not know who is buying from you

What do you need to open new account and how long new account consider new.

1. Need passport valid
2. Need address
3. Need local phone for the same country
4. Need SSN for USA or tax id
5. Need computer
6. Printer
7. Packaging
8. Supplier or products to sell
9. Ink for printer
10. Tape for packaging
11. Need to know where the post office.
12. Need camera, even phone camera is fine to start.
13. Need access to the internet.
14. Storage
15. Paper to print slips.
16. Envelops to pack products
17. Bubbles
18. Need many feedback
19. Has to be open at least a year, otherwise easy to lose account
20. Learn drop ship
21. Work on increasing limits to sell more, always sell 90 to 100 of what your Limit let's you.
22.

EBay only specific questions

1. **Auctions versus fix price –**
   Some times auction makes sense some times fix price makes sense
   Auction is good if you want to find out actual market value of the product and
   see how much interest item will bring.
   Fix price is easier to deal with because you check your account only when
   someone buys, do not have to worry that your auction will end and item will
   sell at the price lower than what you pay for it. Of course you can have
   starting bid at the minimum that you willing to sell for, but than you will have
   almost no following because item already priced in and no reason to bit on it
   for buyers they do not have a feeling that they can steal item bellow value,
   only when people caught up in the bidding that is the time when they over bid
   to get what they want, that is very much impulsive purchases.

2. **Dashboard on EBay.** Very useful tool on EBay where you can find most
   important navigations tools

3. **Platinum titanium statuses**
   That is a status on Amazon that shows that you sell for a few hundred thousands
   per month consistently for 2 -3 years, I will add here exact current regulations,
   but those regulations update constantly. My advice try to grow your business to
   platinum titanium levels as soon as you can. Lot's of credibility that brings to
   sales.

4. **Power seller status**
   Great status on EBay, try to get it as soon as possible. With that status you will
   have more sales and more respect from buyers, I will add here current
   requirements for powerseller shortly, meanwhile you can check it yourself in
   account. If you call customer service they would gladly tell you what you are
   missing in order to become one. Number of sales like 200 per one year, and over
   2000 in sales per year, and proper policy

5. **Understanding bidders**
   You need to try to understand your bidders when you sell, why they bid, why so
   much and not more, when do they bid? Timing during the day for bids. I think
   best auctions end at night on the Sunday, because it gives time everyone who is
   home to spend time and bid. 7 day auctions are the best I think because they are
   not too long like a month, no one wants to wait for the item for a month, and at
   the same time not too short as one day when you get no change to create large
   amount of bidders to increase chance of war for the item between buyers.

6. **Collectables**
   EBay was made perfectly for collectables, if you know any special information
   about collectables you can make money on EBay, visit a few flea markets and
   garage sales perhaps you can find some steal deals. Tough business although

because it requires to list each item separate, write separate new descriptions for each item. Manage insurance and worry that you can send original one way and receive fake on the back if you offer returns. It is very difficult to prove your case. Build up your feedback for more credibility.

7. Unpaid items on eBay

There is a policy that protects sellers on EBay against unpaid items, it is very difficult to enforce, let's say you will force buyer to pay for the item, then they might find a way to be about anything to be un happy and give you negative feedback. It is not fair because eBay can charge you fee for the item, and they get a chance to give you negative feedback even without paying for the item. So my advice, leave it alone, you can write them once or twice politely send them invoice as eBay requires and forget about it.

8.

Amazon specific questions

1. **Fulfillment shipping**- needs to pack solid, follow all instructions on amazon.com, and send to few locations for faster deliveries across the country. Follow up on shipments, print labels yourself, save yourself a buck, pack and put slips on top.

2. **Fulfillment returns** – if fulfillment does not like your goods ask them to ship products back, it will always will be some that they think are wrong. Get it back and repackage if needed and sell yourself.

3. **Fulfillment damaged**- I think they may damage some on purpose, but I find always some that are damaged no matter how well I pack them. Calculate that in your expenses.

4. **Fulfillment packaging, labels, shipping**
Keep a copy for your records, you can kill shipments that are going in far sides of the country and are too costly. Even though amazon.com fulfillment breaks your products in many sets that could be change try different amounts in the first screen. Lets say 200 peaces would be broken as 20 items, 50 items 80 items and 50 items, you do not want to send only 20 or 80 is too much in one shipment, you can kill that particular shipment.

5. **Amazon prime** – great service allows you to receive many goods with now shipping cost for 99 dollars a year great service if you buy a lot on amazon.com
6. **EAN numbers** – are unique numbers that helps to identify products in the world systems

7. **Amazon versus eBay**
You can sell at higher prices on amazon.com then on ebay.com, amazon.com has a bit more stricter policy. You can do fulfillment on Amazon but not on EBay, Amazon fees are higher than EBay fees, regulations on Amazon are stricter, some products sells better on Amazon

8. **Buying Amazon and eBay shares for the shareholder meeting.**
You can buy at least one share of Amazon and one share of eBay so you get invited to shareholder meetings and present your ideas and meet corporate management, see what shareholders are talking, perhaps get some answers to your questions. Get a picture with Jeff Bezo and other important people at the shareholder meetings.

9. **Amazon wars**
Try not to fight with anyone online because both of you can end up losers, wars are costly, you both can end up loosing accounts.

10. Assign ASIN

Try to assign your own new ASIN that way you will not be in conflict with other sellers. Get an ASIN the earlier the better, that way you will have more time to make your product searchable online.

11. Other people adding pictures to your listing on Amazon

Amazon allows other people to add pictures to your listings that is mostly a good thing because after you upload 9 pictures on Amazon you are done, but you can send some pictures to your buyers, friends and other partners and they can add more pictures of your product if that is necessary.

12. Links to Amazon

It is great to idea to create many links to your Amazon page, that would put you in much higher search results. The more links you have to your page on Amazon, the more love you will see from Amazon. Try to ask friends with websites and partners to create back links to your store.

13. Reports from Amazon

There are many reports that Amazon create by itself and there even more reports that you can order and they would be generated in anywhere like a day to two weeks. Great tool for someone who loves statistics and numbers. I do not have time to deal with that, because it is a part time business for me for now but I see great value in those reports.

14. Pre fulfillment cancellations

I hate when it happens, but that is life and it is better to get your final fee back rather than spend money on shipping, site fees and than get in a fight with buyer. 15.

Security

1. **How to make your account separate so others can not log in and kill your account.**
a. Try to get as many feedbacks as possible. You need at least 100 positive feedbacks for one negative that you might encounter so your account would stay top rated and in compliant.
b. Try to be fully legitimates, compliant
c. Sell legal products,
d. Protect your brand
e. Use your own listing do not stand behind someone else, because other sellers work hard to create good listing and will try to protect it from you making profits on their sweat.

2. **How to protect your account**
Call tech support often, make a human interaction, that you are real person and interact with ebay.com and amazon.com, have many positive feedbacks so even if you get few bad once from the competitor friends, you will not be knocked out.

3. **Fraud cases** – try to recognize fraud in advance. In case of ebay.com fraud often comes from new sellers, not because those are actually new sellers but because those accounts have been specifically created to steal from you. Make sure that you have insurance on expensive items. Make sure that you contact buyers before sending suspicious orders. If someone over sudden buys from you un usually large amount of the product, contact the person. Feel it. Find the explanation. Be worry. Understand the logic behind purchases. Be concern with international shipping and un usual countries. I find that people in European countries are more eager to cancel payment and give negative feedback in order to get stuff for free than in economies like USA or Canada. But I may be wrong.

4. **Competition fraud:** if you have popular product that sells well you risk that competitors will try to close your business without letting you to smell the profit. Or to make your life more difficult. See who is buying from you, make sure addresses are real, and when many bad feedbacks comes at once, that is probably an orchestrated attack by the competitor who wants to take you out of business. You can call amazon.com and ebay.com and explain your situation, explain if the addresses are fictitious, if the phone numbers are not real, if the behavior out of the ordinary. See what they are selling, attack probably comes from the accounts that specifically created for that purposes, not sellers account to prevent retaliation. I would say bad peace is better than major war. War will hurt you and your competitors, try to find common ground. Market is large, should space for everyone. When negative feedbacks are too long they can make a

mistake and write the same feedback word for word from different accounts or copy popular negative feedbacks from online communities and paste to hurt you. You can point that out to the customer service rep at amazon.com and at ebay.com that that is not a genuine feedback but a copy to hurt you. It is more difficult to fight when feedback is just one word like FAKE. Service reps will tell you that customers are entitle to the opinion. I would not recommend to engage in fight with every crazy person online. Do your think that not stepping on others feet, make it so it would be difficult to copy you and to be in your arena. Sell more and have more positive feedback so even if you get some negative you can move on. Have 1000 positive on each negative.

5. Your employees

You can have dedicated staff to respond to emails if you have many orders to track and respond. When you ship over 1000 items per day, it makes sense to put someone just to respond to orders. You can have listing employer who would write great descriptions and do photography and review writing.

You can have another employee who would do shipping and packaging, going to post office and ship boxes.

Audit of the stock shelf. You can hire someone to do market research for you even part time if you can not afford someone on staff full time.

6.

Money

1. PayPal payments

Are quite convenient, and accepted all over the world. Some countries like Ukraine for instance right now does not allow to receive payments via PayPal but allows to send payments.

Problems with paypal.com are fees, that paypal.com is always on the side of the buyer and with any request will send the money back to sender. Also money on paypal.com clears slowly, it can take up to 24 days to clear fully payment. Paypal.com will send money that you receive even 60 days after the transaction. So just because you send stuff and receive payments and got feedback, it is not over yet, you still can have some attrition of the funds even after 45 days since sale. You paypal.com should mirror your ebay.com account in terms of address, phone, credit card info and etc. if you lose your paypal.com account so goes your ebay.com account, I would say paypal.com account is more important than ebay.com account

2. Verifying PayPal

With active phone, proper address, and all matching information it is easy to verify information for PayPal,

3. PayPal policy

Always on the side of the buyer

If you send money person to person you can save on fees, the minute it becomes business than 2 percent and higher, on large numbers it can add up.

4. **Taxes, forward invoices** Like any other business here in the USA online sales require to pay taxes, especially if you sell in your state, you should file state and federal taxes. Get a good accountant who can help you do the right thing by yourself, and IRS. That is why keep all your expenses that you can write off. Cost of wrapping paper, printer, tonner, ink, cost of internet, cost of gas and amortization on your car for caring boxes to post office, bags for shipping boxes, computer, camera, photo studio, cost of goods from suppliers. Etc, your accountant would know better that can be written off and what is un reasonable. Be reasonable

5. Refunds

Refunds are bad, but not that bad, you should count at least each 10th transaction that can go wrong, it will always be customers who would want things for free and ask for refund. It possible to fight that and not to sell to them in a future on EBay but on Amazon, to our pity it is part of business for now. Try to see if they can take partial refund, at least to pay for 50 percent or not to refund shipping and taxes. Worth comes to worth, give money back, your feedback rating is more important than one item, I hope the cost of each item in your stock not that expensive. That is one of the reasons why we mostly work with cheap items because even if problem arise it is easier to give money back and forget about it.

6. Pricing
Setting pricing is a tricky thing, you need to calculate all your expenses, when you start and have tiny sales, you would probably sell and would not be able to cover all the expenses, consider that as your starting expenses for the business. It is like opening restaurant and wanting to get your money back from first few customers, it takes time to build up reputation, establish reviews, feedback, follow up. Consider your first few months as educational curve.

7. First two years of business
This is the time to learn about EBay and Amazon, that is the time to establish feedback, not to lose your account, not to caught up in negative feedbacks and navigate from infant account and selling online knowledge to become someone who can manage business. Try to read as many books on the subject as you can, try to meet many other sellers and pick their brains.

8. Tax id
It is important to have separate tax it for your online business from your social so in case account get's closed you will not loose your personal ability to sell online

9. Bank account to receive funds
Have bank accounts in major banks; link your account to the online business so Amazon can pay you directly. In case your bank account gets compromise, change it right away.

10. Variable closing fees
Both EBay and Amazon have many variable closing fees that are not easily recognizable, watch out for them. Be not surprise they are there.

11. Financing circle
Some business have great sales in Christmas time, be ready with products, some products like New Year calendars sell well before new year. Be prepared with stock of product in advance, but not too much in advance. Understand your seasons, and how fast money moves from one product to next.

12. Insuring your online business
Once your business becomes big and reliable source or even main source of your income, it is time to think about insuring your business. There are self insurance, there friends and family members who can insure and there are official ways to do so. You can consider Buy Sell agreements and you can consider Key Employee insurance. You can read about those policies with insurance companies and talk to your personal insurance specialist.

13. Forms for taxes

14. Amazon and EBay do forms automatically in January for tax purposes usually you will get tax forms if you sell more than 20k worth of goods in a given year. Just bring forms that you print from the website to your account with your expenses and notes and accountant will do the job. I am not license CPA so I do not give advice on taxes

15. Business model

Figure out what is your business model, how you will make more, selling individual items or try to sell in bulk, go for quality of product or volume. Variety of products or few concentrated products, top to bottom approach or bottom to top approach.

16. Selling personal versus business

When you sell as personal account you never can re open your account, on the other side if business account would be closed, it does not mean that you never can open personal EBay account.

Businesses pay more in taxes but personal accounts are more liability, let's say if you sell product like cosmetic and it damage someone famous face and they can not get work because of your cosmetics and in case they win that case in court, you can be liable for large amounts, but if that is business selling account it could be just bankruptcy for business not for you personally.

17. Carrying cost

Is the cost how much it cost you to carry product, what did you pay for the product, your monthly fee let's say to Amazon for the store front and your storage fee and your fee in general to run the business. See what it cost you actually.

18. Cash flow

Manage your cash flow, always see how much money are coming from sales versus what you putting in, try to have positive cash flow at all times, the more you make, the more invest, not the other way. See the relationship on those two rivers, you do not want to be stock with a lot of stuff that you can not sell later on. Of course mistakes would be made and wrong product for sale would be purchased by you, but try not to see too much of it.

19. Inventory

Try not to have too much in inventory, but at the same time not to low, plan in advance of holidays, consider items that can sell out to pre order from suppliers in large amounts or more often shipments

20. Buying on credit card

I see once in a while when the whole business could be run on credit cards. That business of online is so fast if you have the right product that you can sell your products so fast that you will pay no interest or little interest. People who say that they can not start small online business because they do not have cash, are wrong, as long as you have business, viable business you can run it on credit cards, just be on top of things and pay all cards on time. Credit is a great thing for online sellers like us.

21. PayPal limits
Initially PayPal will give you small limits like 1000 dollars and but as you verify your account and time goes by and you get more and more payments to the account your limits will increase. Just keep password to PayPal really tightly safe. Work on increasing your limits and move money from PayPal to your bank account as soon as substantial amount will be there, leave some balance so you have money to spend for the business purposes, pay from the PayPal balance, that way some funds never reach your bank account and that is leaves some room for your accountant to interpret transactions in your favor, do not play with IRS but be smart about it. Do it legal way.

22. Seller limits
When you start selling on EBay your limits are to 200 dollars and to 10 items, as time goes by your seller limits increase, allows you to sell more

23. Insuring sales

24. Escrow scam

25. FIFO
First item that you purchase is sold first
That way you have kind of fare amount of shelf time for all products.
That method is good for people who want move the shelf, so no product would not get too old.

26. LIFO last in first out
Accounting method that allows you to pay taxes and manage your business in the following setting. Last item that you purchase for sale you count as the first item that you sell, that way your older products stays longer with you. Great when you dealing with products that require to be fresh, because older product can be outdated and you may want to write them off rather then selling. People who do that care for the feedback and quality and want to sell first best product and worth product leave for the end.

27. Pro forma invoice
28. **Profits calculate all expenses in** – when you do your taxes calculate all expenses. Calculate the amortization of your car, oil for car, printer, computer, camera, light, calculate all expenses, do not add what is not there but be fair.

29. **Margins on products**- what percentage of profit you make on particular item, I like to have at least 4 dollar profit per item to make my business interesting.

Let's say I buy item on aliexpress.com at the cost of 1 dollar per item, it cost me to ship it 2 dollars including packaging and 1 dollar fee goes to ebay.com that way I spend 1 dollar out of the pocket sell it at 8 dollars and made 4 dollars, I find that is a good business. Also consider fraud expense, that is also additional 10 percent loss.

30. **Return on investment**- you need to know your total expenses and how much profit it brings you. How much did you invest in that business, products, supply of packaging, paper and etc, and how much did you actually made after all expenses.

31. **Taking partners**- is the last resort, as long as you can run business yourself, have friends, sell separate, but the minute you take partners you open up for many problems and disputes.

32. **Loans** – if you certain that business is solid and products selling fast you can borrow money even on credit cards, or loans from banks, friends or your savings, or from your home equity. I do not like lending for small business, I tend to operate small and grow as profits show more money and leave funds in business pull but some times you may need to take a risk or take a partner which is also risk.

33. **Sell through rate** – that is a rate of what sells and what is not and how fast you can sell particular product, how fast your money after investing in product comes back to you.

34. **Selling at cost or bellow**- there are cases when it makes sense to sell at cost or even bellow cost in order to grow account to power seller or to increase your selling limits on the new accounts. Sometimes when you enter the market and acquisition of the new items is more expensive than selling it, but that would give you understanding if it makes sense to penetrate that market on larger scale.
Also you may choice to sell at cost or bellow to acquire more feedback and fix your score faster if you got bad feedback and you want it to go away on the page, than I would buy some products from 99 cents store and sell at cost or even at a loss, in order to get many good positive feedbacks and move the bad feedback to second page.

35. **Store credit**- sometimes instead of returning funds you can offer clients store credit to buy something else let's say at different proportion, like 100 to 110 percent that way instead of giving out real money you will sell more product, perhaps at slightly more expensive cost of acquisition.

36. **Supply and demand** – that is what moves the market on amazon.com and ebay.com you can research what sells more and where higher profits and

where not that much competition and based on your analysis decide what to buy and sell and when to do so.

37. **Leasing equipment** – storage in Manhattan for example cost quite a bit but some times you have to be in the right place, so you can lease or rent space rather than buying, same goes for leasing computer, color laser printer, fancy camera for jewelry photo shoot.

38. Bookkeeping

Do your numbers yourself but at some point you may need more of outside help. Keep all the receipts that you spend, keep all the charges, keep excel spread shit.

39. Consignment

The more you work with supplier for more they would trust you. Perhaps some of them can give you there product on consignment and expect that you will be fair and pay them back later on when you sell their product. It is great way of increasing your stock without putting any money upfront.

Images and pictures for EBay and Amazon notes by Alexander Gurman 2014

1. **Photography, requirements, regulations, white background**
Amazon.com requires high quality pictures with many pick cells and so does ebay.com now. Post as many pictures as you can, let's say 9 on amazon.com and 12 on ebay.com for free. On amazon.com others can add more pictures to your listing as buyers. Have your product viewed from different positions, front, side, upper, from the bottom. Amazon.com requires white background on all pictures, it will still publish other backgrounds, but you will lose points in search and will be not as highly visible as someone else in same category with white background pictures. Do not have other objects in the pictures. Do not have labels on the pictures. Title your pictures so the name of your product and store will be in. Try not to have black space in the picture title; it is not good for indexing your page by the search engines.

2. **Taking pictures of the small objects.** Taking pictures of small objects is difficult to get it really clear. You may need tripod so your camera would not shake. Get as close to item as lenses would allow you. Try to make pictures with good light, look at the camera monitor often to see what you are getting done. Play with settings, start with auto and than go to manual if you know how to use it. Try to have light from a both sides and from the back of the object, do not have clutter in the picture of un necessary products.

3. **Properly labeling your images and videos.**
When you label your images call them the same name as product or your user name that way it will lead to you and give you more exposure online, every time your name is revoked online or clicked your rating online goes up and you become more searchable. That is very important, for the website creating it is important not to have black spaces in the titles of your images so use under score if you need to segregate words

4. **Cropping image**
Remove from the image all the sides that are not necessary for the sale, all extra stuff that you had in the room when you too picture is not necessary, crop your pictures.

5. **Clutter in image**
When you have too much details and additional things in the image that is not good. I understand that you want to show a coin to demonstrate the size, but some buyers will ask for the coin to be included in the purchase. You even can have some product on the female model in the picture and someone may ask you why they did not receive actual model in addition to the product. People sometimes are very straight thinkers and narrow minded, in order to avoid confusion, just take picture of your product, at least have just the product on the first three pictures that you upload, including the main picture

6. Software for the image control

Perhaps Adobe Photoshop would be the best choice for windows folks but for the basic needs any software even free software that comes with camera or computer will do the trick. You would need very basic functions like crop and resize and those functions are available in even the free software.

7. File size of image

Try to have file size as big as you can up to 2 3 megabytes, perhaps 30 meg is way to big as new cameras or video cameras can produce too large files, they are tough to work with on older computers, try to have as clear as possible image but not wasting to much space on the hard drive, remember some people who are your buyers have very old slow computers with weak internet signal so for they your pictures will load for a long time and so they may go else where. Try to have best quality and size and quality some times goes together.

8. Lightning

Have lights reflectors from a variety angles, that way you will have picture like in 3D, have a lot of light, you can always reduce light but if not enough light you are in trouble. Have flash from different angles not directly on the object, that way object would not be flat. Natural day light is probably the best but if you take pictures after work at night and online selling is second hobby of yours, that is fine.

9. Tripod use for the picture quality, even little movements of the camera and shaky hands can damage your picture when you shoot small items with an average camera that is not specific lenses for the item photography.

10. Have some
11. Overexposure in light
12. register to sell stock photography of your products and other pictures that would establish you as stock photography legal seller
13. can sell your images as well
14.

15. Amazon rules for images

Every product on Amazon needs one or more product image. The primary image of your item is called the "MAIN." The MAIN image represents an item in search results and browse pages and is the first image customers see on a product detail page.

Images are very important to customers, so quality matters. Images must accurately represent the product and show only the product that's for sale, with minimal or no propping. Choose images that are clear, easy to understand, information-rich, and attractively presented.

Image standards
Images must accurately represent the product and show only the product that's for sale, with minimal or no propping.
MAIN images must have a pure white background (pure white blends in with the Amazon search and item detail pages - RGB values of 255, 255, 255).
MAIN images must show the actual product (not a graphic or illustration), and must NOT show excluded accessories, props that may confuse the customer, text that is not part of the product, or logos/watermarks/inset images.
The product must fill 85% or more of the image.
Images should be 1000 pixels or larger in either height or width, as this will enable zoom function on the website (zoom has proven to enhance sales). The smallest your file should be is 500 pixels on the longest side.
Amazon accepts JPEG (.jpg), TIFF (.tif), or GIF (.gif) file formats. JPEG is preferred.
Additional images
MAIN images should be supplemented with additional images showing different sides of a product, the product in use, or details that aren't visible in the MAIN image.
A white background is recommended, but not required. Additional images must not include logos or watermarks, and all props or accessories must be presented in a way that do not cause customer confusion.
Note: Our servers cannot accept images that are not formatted to our specifications. In addition, we reserve the right to remove images that do not meet our image standards. It is your responsibility to ensure that you have all necessary rights for the images you submit.

There is a mistake on a product detail page. How can I correct it?

The information displayed on a product detail page may be drawn from multiple seller contributions. The information you have contributed about a product may or may not be displayed. This decision is processed automatically according to business logic known as Detail Page Control. Detail Page Control determines which of the seller-submitted product descriptions, features, titles, and additional details are displayed on the product detail page.

Product information
To fix or improve product information on a product detail page, try one of these options:

•Go to Manage Inventory and click the item's Actions link, then select Edit details.
•Upload an inventory file that includes the updated product info.

If your contribution is approved, it will appear immediately on the product detail page.
•From the product detail page on Amazon.com, scroll down to Product Details, and click the "Tell us what we missed" link.
If your contribution is approved, it will appear on the detail page within 3 business days.
If your change is not approved or you need further assistance, contact Seller Support, and select "Inventory" then "Wrong information on product pages."

Product images
To fix or improve a product image, use one of these options:

•Go to Manage Inventory, click the Actions link for the SKU, and then select Manage product images.
•Upload an inventory file that includes an image URL.
•Go to Amazon.com, locate your product, scroll down to Product Details, and then click the "Give feedback on images" link. (You cannot upload a new image from this location.)

Additional Corrections
If the corrections you want to submit are not supported by Manage Inventory or inventory file upload, or if there is incorrect information that you cannot remove, contact Seller Support, and select "Inventory" then "Wrong information on product pages."

Publishers, filmmakers, and music labels use Vendor Central to update and enhance their product listings.

How can we improve this Help page? Wrong information Missing information Confusing information (Optional) Enter your suggested improvement here. If you need help, skip this field and click the Contact Seller Support button. Submit
We appreciate your feedback. Thank you.
There is a mistake on a product detail page. How can I correct it?
When will I see my products on Amazon.com?
How do I edit my listing and product information?
When and how do I list a back-ordered product?
Product Categories and Stores
Using UPCs

Model Release

In consideration of _____ or /and_____ share of profits from photo and video produced, I,

_____, do
hereby give _____ for _____, assigns,
licensees, and legal representatives the irrevocable right to use my image
in all forms and media and in all manners, including composite and
distorted representations, for advertising, trade, or any other lawful
purposes, and I waive any rights to inspect or approve the finished
product, including written copy ant may be created in connection
therewith. The following name may be used in reference to these
photographs, videos:
My real name or

_____
Short Description of photographs, videos:

_____
Additional information:
Please Print: Name _____
Address _____
City _____ State _____ Zip code _____
County _____
Phone_____ Email _____

Consent (if model is under the age of 18) I am the parent or guardians of
the minor named above and have the legal authority to execute the above
release. I approve the foregoing and waive any rights in the premises.

Please print. Name _____
Address _____
City _____ State _____ Zip code _____
County _____

Signature _____
Witness _____ Date

Your name
Address
Contact information

Advertising

1. **Why one sells others do not:** there are many factors involved and still to the end I would not know some times. Here are factors that can affect,
a. Better pictures than yours,
b. Better description, more in detail
c. Older account than yours, old accounts tent to show better in search
d. Accounts with more listing than ours, they just get more visits from browsing buyers.
e. Higher feedback rating
f. Better feedback score
g. Better policy compliance
h. More key words, more meta tags, or better key words, better meta tags
i. More advertisement on google ads, and amazon adds, better website, better grammar
j. Free shipping
k. Offer international shipping
l. 30 or 60 or even 90 days money back guarantee
m. More sold items put buyers at ease
n. Name of the seller also matter, pick good name that people want to buy from
o. Listings with many sold items and few available trigger desire to buy now.
p. The order of those factors is not necessarily the most correct order, at the next revision I will try to list them in more orderly fashion

2. **Marketing of the products**
You can advertise on google.com

3. **Advertising on Google**
It is not that expensive, create account link it to your other google account, you would need an email address that other than gmail.com think yahoo, hotmail, etc
Start with small budget, use free coupon to start, google.com offer from 50 to 150 in advertising credits to start account. You can start with as little as 50 dollars campaign.
Advertising on google.com has other benefits, products become more searchable and you will come up in organic search as well, one of the things that you want out of the campaign is that to become searchable better than competitors. So choice the right key words and start adverting.
Customer service folks will help you for free to understand the system and make better ads. Do not overspend, try some and see results, after a while you can stop and see the difference if it worth to continue to advertise

4. **Advertising on Amazon**
Really helps you to advance your product rating on the site, even with small budget you get more listing power than other places where you can spend money on promotion

5. Advertising on facebook.com
In my experience not that much productive for the products that I sell, but it can work for you if you are in word of mouth business and need exposure among mostly young folks.
Obviously have a page for your products on facebook.com and run the discussion alive there.

6. Likes power
50 likes gives you power to appear on others page, try to get as many likes as possible, likes are powerful in sense that they stay and show how popular are you to others. Keep in mind that likes on facebook.com and amazon.com are distinctly different likes and you need both.

7. **Media like news papers and magazines, radio and TV** with regard to advertisement your products to sell on ebay.com and amazon.com

8. **Logo** – your logo is very important to get right, it has to be easy to load, right size and proper dimensions. Look official and simple and at the same time different from major brands, you can use your given name that would be difficult to compete and take away from you by the big brands. Letters easy or symbols are quite recognizable. Try if you can get a professional advice from graphic designer or painter or some kind of artist with taste. Do not put a lot of money in.

9. **Key words** – are important, they have to relevant to your product, if the key words are popular but not relevant it also helps to bring up your product but if ebay.com and amazon.com will find out that you have that practice, and they will, you will be severely penalize, that is not fair practice so try to stay in relevant search key words.

10. **Tags** – are important in use to get more exposure and to be better found over twitter and facebook.com and other places.

11. GoDaddy.com
Great website to buy domain name and basic website development, they have great support and most of questions would answered for you. I am using right now mostly readyhosting.com but no longer because they are the best, but because I used to them and 15 years ago I started with them and I have many websites on their platform and know it and I not like to study all the time for new things, I try to concentrate on making money on what I know already.

12. Google ad words
Google ad words is probably the most effective way to advertise that I have found for my new products, it is great for EBay and Amazon sellers especially if you create your own products and promote them online, even for the existing

products it is a great tool. Open account, call for customer service, and decide what kind of campaign you want to run. Calculate your budget. You can start with as little as 50 dollars budget. You can use free promotional 100 dollar code that all of us getting from Google in the mail. You can pay for the clicks or for expressions, I like to pay for clicks and I put my own cost to it, half of the what is suggested that way I do not over spend when I start new advertising campaign, choice key words and you are in business. You can monitor statistics and see what is working and what is not.

13. Google add sense

That is a service when you post videos on YouTube and other video services and get paid for advertisement that run on your videos. Great way to find out what is your targeted audience. If you talented you can make some money on the side, some people make it really big but very few.

14.

Amazon.com and Ebay.com lessons how to sell
Other sites where we sell are etsy.com overstock.com

1. How to sell

Sell a lot of good for good prices and sell fast and get awesome top rating feedback. How to do that you will learn in my notes here. I do not know every secret and every trick but I will share what I know and some private really valuable advices I can sell in private for separate fee (also some of the ideals that I know are not originally mine and I would get permission from the person who share the knowledge with me in each case it would be individual deal, individual prices. Please feel free to inquire about special deal for you) Alexander@AlexGurman.com

2. **What to have for the ebay.com** and amazon.com business: measuring tape, weights for small weight, camera, perhaps studio for photos, shipping tape, shipping tape holder, perhaps large and small sizes, have some envelops, boxes, have a reliable computer and printer and back up computer and printer in case of virus and broken equipment. Have all your listing saved on the removable hard drive, in case you get a virus, you will save your product picture library and product descriptions.

3. **Checking performance**- check your feedback and performance constantly to see your weak spots and to have a chance to fix problems before they become serious peace that affects business.

4. **Price management with competition**-
   You can lower your prices and that would make your competitors angry if your prices will be way lower than the rest of sellers in the product line, I would suggest not to be the lowest and do not be most expensive, just be second lowest if you want to sell large quantity and be a bit in the middle if you want to start getting good serious customers.

5. **Closed accounts**- can not be ever re open to my knowledge amazon.com and ebay.com do not revisit those discussions so stay away from losing your accounts. Try to comply with every request that amazon.com will make in order to keep account open, put account on ice, stop selling improve the rating on good products but do not get your accounts closed.

6. Selling from your website

Everything that you sell on ebay.com and amazon.com you should sell on your website and even more. Since you own website you do not have to put negative complains public and you can avoid ebay.com and amazon.com fees since you can sell directly. The benefit of selling on amazon.com and ebay.com is because those two sites right now hold the majority of the buyer's traffic and are very trustworthy on the client side, so people are not afraid to buy there.

7. Domain parking

With godaddy.com you can buy some domains that relate to your business and that way control the traffic on the products that goes in your seller category. Have key words in name. Prefer .com to any other extension. Try to have those short titles not too long, use common meaningful words easy to spell. Do not use abbreviations, since simple words are by now mostly taken, you can add something short to make it distinct like thegroomingbook.com or BargeFishing.com or FishingBaitGlue.com

You can use your last name and first name if they are good in sound, that domain could be very difficult to take away from you. Like alexgurman.com or svitlanaholovko.com that way you will advertise yourself and it would be more difficult to close your account.

8. Keeping notes

Keep notes on what sells, and what works in your business, keep lists of bad buyers who steal from you,

9. Having many accounts

Is a great ideal for many reasons?
   a. Segregate different businesses
   b. If one account happen to be closed others will survive
   c. The negative aspect here is that you share feedback between many accounts; it does not go in one large feedback rating.
   d. If one account will receive a few negative feedback or warnings or violations, you can put that account on ice and sell from other accounts, because after 6 months or year depends on the case, negative feedbacks will go away and will less hurt your ratings. If you continue to sell on that account you may lose the account for good.

   10. **Block bad buyers from you**, from being able to buy more and steal more from you, you can share a list of bad buyers and share with other sellers and they can give you their block lists in return

11. Top seller secrets

I am sharing my secrets here.
I will develop this section as we go along

International accounts

You can open accounts for many countries

12. Accounts from Ukraine Russia

Those questions I usually answer for separate fee on one on one basis. If you interested in that particular topic, it would be best to discuss that in private my email is Alexander@AlexGurman.com or cell is 917 825 8225, thank you for the understanding but that kind of information worth more than what I charge for the book.

13. Opening accounts with others
You can give your account to someone for the management, by giving them user name and password on personal accounts you would be able to still control account

You can ask your friends and family members to open accounts as well and sell from their name, of course proper compensation is in order, and usually people pay from 5 to 15 percent for the use of the account. 10 percent is most common agreement type. That is the case when

14. Other Amazon competing sites.
Bonanza.com Overstock.com Etsy.com Ozon.ru in Russia, They are all are viable solutions, just with tiny market right now and niche market, try them, who to say that one day would not be bigger than their big brothers now. Just consider time and effort, do not spread yourself too thin between many platforms, learn one or two and become professional and expert on it.

15. Variety of products to increase traffic
I would recommend having many different products even if you sell just one product because that can increase traffic to your store, because you will be searchable my many organic key words.

16. Automation
Try to bring automation to your business as much as you can, that can save you time. Packaging, have all in one place so you do not wonder around your house looking for tape, printer, product. Have required instruments like spare paper, spare cartridge for printer, scissors and other peaces where you have them every day. Like park your car same place if you can, so next day you do not have look for it.

17. Templates, keeping files on computer for each listing
Keep all templates on your computer for each listing or on the drop box online so you can access them in case of need later on. Title them the way that you can find them again in time

18. Organizing your computer database
Have a basic database of your stock, of your documents and your suppliers, your buyers. You may need those for tax purposes or for internal analyzes. If you will not have to re picture your products after a while because you can not find some files, that can be bit time savior.

19. Evaluation metrics
There are a vast list of resources that allows you to see how well did you do. You can see visitors per page, you can see customer satisfaction, you can study how fast different post services deliver your goods. Watch your metrics and try to see up beat performance, see more sales on monthly base and you will be fine.

20. Selling in bulk
Sometimes it is good sell in bulk, that way you can move a lot of product and even small profit but on volume can me big money. Also it will drastically reduce your costs as purchaser, and you can get more free samples from suppliers who want to you to sell their products.

21. Educating clients about products
It is important to explain your products to clients that way they would no how to properly use the product and you will have less complains. Also educated client would understand why to buy products from you rather than your competitors because your clients would know your story.

22. Writing product instructions and manual how to install and use.
On new products that you make yourself and receive from suppliers without proper instructions and manual, I would recommend to write instructions and manual and include in the package, will save you a lot of time and perhaps few un necessary complains.

23. Establishing selling goals.
Before you start a project, create for yourself goals how much you want to make, how much you want to sell, where your business should be in a months from now, quarter, a year, 5 years and see if you can follow you plan, that is important to know if your business makes sense. You do not want to work for nothing, that would help you to stay on right course.

24. Craigslist.org
Great place to sell stuff locally, research what is out there, find help, find local product to sell online. Some items like used cars I think sells better on craigslist than on EBay.

25. Product condition new versus used, or damaged
There are people who like to buy new products and there are those who like to buy used stuff at deep discount. There is market for both, EBay and Amazon is great for those used products

26. Brand rules.
No one likes to buy generic, very little trust, people like brands to try to sell brand product or at least create a brand.

27. Repeat purchases
It is wonderful to get repeat business from customers, try to find out why they buy products from you and try to sell more often, perhaps a discount can make sense if you get consistent buyer. Like my customers who like to buy fishing bait glue from me, are buying when jar is empty. The more they fish, the more they buy.

28. **Business cards to include in each order.**
It is a good practice to have business card in every order. You will get more repetitive business and people who will buy from you will have more respect to your business as establish business rather than someone who look to rip them off by buying somewhere cheap and sell to you high.

29. **Discussion board**- many good and free advice could found on discussion boards, if you have time to hang out there you may find suggestions on what to sell and what is more important what not to sell and why. On new regulations and other seller tricks and ideas. You can find strategic partnerships on those boards.

30. **Checking your history of transactions** – that is what you should do on paypal.com, amazon.com and on ebay.com important to know where money left your account, what fees came due, how long it took to clear your money.

31. **Sleeping accounts** for the future business establish to have longer dates. You can open accounts for your relatives and friends and if you have not enough of product and time to sell from those accounts, you still should open as many as you can and leave accounts in the sleep mode. First of all there is no free to have accounts open on those sites. Second, the older the account, the more respectful business and higher limitation on things that you can do on old accounts. Always try to have many accounts, ready to take over in case you start selling more than your account let's you.

32. **Your own website and links**
Try to have your user name on Amazon and on EBay the same as your website that way people who search for you specifically or want to buy directly from you without Amazon and EBay fees can find you on Google quite easily.

33. **Research on competition**
Obviously do your research on competition, find out how long they do that, where are they physically located. What products do they sell, how they sell, how they advertise so you do not have to re invent business, learn from them. May be there is room for partnership, may be it is too dangerous business for you to get in so you should avoid entering it because niche is tightly managed.

34. **Sales categories, proper categories**
There are proper categories on Amazon and on EBay where products should be listed, some times there are border categories when you can list in one or the other, see what one is more appropriate. Some times it makes sense to list in both or more other categories.

35. **Shopzilla.com**
Shopzilla.com is another website where you can sell, not as popular as Amazon and EBay but also a place to be if you have time.

36. Skype
Great, free mostly tool to communicate with your buyers, suppliers and partners online; you can message and watch and talk in real time. You can use your smart phone to speak via Skype and show your products to clients via Skype. Great tool, use it , it is still not as clear as phone but still major saving in communications. Addition to email and phone big time.

37. Social network websites
Great place to promote your products, not that much as actual sales, but still good for creating value and brand and following. Do not spend to much time and effort on those yet. Its power highly overstated in the media for folks like us who just want to sell on EBay and Amazon. Be real.

38. Face book, odnoklasniki link in, kontact.ru
Facebook.com market place is a great place to spread word around if you have large network, Odnoklasniki.ru is very popular site for Russian speaking folks to share information and promote products via groups
Linkedin.com is major website that is made for professional communications.

39. Stamps.com
Great place to print shipping labels, and buy stamps on discount and print your own labels online. I actually use right now EBay and Amazon to create new labels, because I am familiar with those but stamps.com is still good resource for large packages.

40. Your store front
Your storefront should correlate with your online business, have your storefront picture online and have picture of your online website on your awnings for business. Have your website on your sign so people can go online and buy from you even at night when they drive by your store or on holidays or after work when your store is closed. Some people would not have time to go inside your store but they would save your website address from the sign and research you on the website before actually walking in the store. Just do it.

41. Kindle register for seller
Right now it is a great time to register your kindle account to sell books on Amazon, it is free, later on perhaps 5 -6 years from now an account like that can worth a few thousand dollars easily based on what happen with accounts that have been allowed to sell in MP3 category or in clothing category, Amazon does not add new seller accounts in those categories and everyone who wants to sell in those categories can not open new accounts but have to go existing sellers or sell in category as others which is not so good searchable as proper categories. Bottom line, open kindle seller account and you may want to use it for business in the future right now they are available and free.

42. Missed promises
There are many missed promises online, slow shipment, wrong product put in the box or wrong size of the items, erroneous descriptions. Try to have as little as possible on your side, always improve your listings and policies, learn on yours and others mistakes. When you get time browse and look for best practices by competitors.

43. Market share
Try to go for big market, than even small share of the market would be a lot of money. Problem here is that it is difficult to get in large market, so I would recommend to not to step on any one else toes, just gain share gradually that way you know dangers that you might face.

44. Return policy
Spell out all your policy requirements, that would help you to get more sales, give clarity what people are signing up with you and what they can expect from you.

45. Product line
Try to have more than one product lines, because what you think will sell may not and something that you think might not sell, will actually sell well. If you starting with one line of business do it well and add all the tags, and links and reviews that can help you to have a peace of business.

46. Prohibited words
There are words that get you in trouble online on EBay and Amazon like words: fake, not authentic, fraud, etc try to avoid typing those words at all cost. Both selling sites have computer programs that search for those words and combinations and penalize you for using those words if you are seller. It may trigger to close you account or get warning.
Do not thread anyone on the sites because they have zero tolerance policy for treats, you will be prevented into even getting into your accounts. Would have no access to money or items. Be very careful what you write, never write in anger, calm down, this is just business, be professional. I for example get grumpy in the morning or late at night after tough day and that can show in my emails especially if I see that person try to take advantage from me. Breath let it go.

47. Ranking in sellers
The hire your ranking is the more sales you can get, into ranking goes many factors, your feedback, your performance, compliance policy, relevancy of your listing, number of sales and etc. check your ranking and try to improve your ranking, even ask Amazon and EBay support people what to do to improve your ranking. More pictures, better quality, more sales.

48. Recommendations
Try to get as many recommendations for your business, for your products as possible, collect them, scan and store properly, you might need them very much

when problem arise with un happy customer. You may want to send them to sites staff to show your serious intentions.

49. Repeat customers

Are the best customers, you already won their trust and now it is time to make more sales to them and their friends, do not be shy and ask for referral to someone who buys the same stuff, offer them coupon discount if their referral would buy from you, it may worth it.

50. Refund rate, good product and bad product in terms of refunds percentage

A good product is a product that does not have very high refund rate, anything less than 10 percent is good. Online market is spoiled by Leonean policies and they like to return for no reason or at least for reasons that are not that important to you as seller. Be patient that is part of doing business on these sites. If you get too many returns that it's affect your business either stops selling this product, or change something in your description.

51. **Leaving your mailing address online** Given all cons and pro in, it makes sense to leave your mailing address online on your site because it gives you more legitimacy as business.

52. **Phone confirmation, online phone numbers** You can take orders on a phone also; just get in email in writing. You would need to have a cell phone for the opening account and will receive a code on the phone. You can get

53. Your fax

Have your fax available at all times online, because you still will find some business comes via fax. The cost of having it so little that it totally worth it to have, you even can have online fax for free that would go to your email.

54. Support groups, partners, team of other sellers

Support groups are important, they would help you with advice and different angle to the problem and perhaps with the solution to your problem. You might need to have partners and sell in the group of sellers because than you are more powerful with suppliers and you together as a group can better understand the market. You can share success and loss stories to prevent future loss and extend future success.

55. Calling for tech support.

Whenever you find a problem, call tech support it is free most of the times with Amazon and EBay and with GoDaddy.com so try to get as much as possible support.

56. Protecting your account from employees

Keep your private information safe away from your employees if they sell for you, if you let someone do customer service for you or shipping or advertising of your products. Try to follow logs who and when log in on account and what kind of activity has been done.

57. Technology

Go with technology, it is not necessary to have the latest camera, latest computer, and latest software as long as it works, does not improve what is working already. Although update your antivirus software

58. Viruses

Viruses on computer are the bitch. Try to avoid them at all cost. Viruses kill the business. Try to avoid visiting bogus websites. Do not go on pornography websites. Do not open unusual attachments, remember that your friends can get a virus and send it to you. Just do not download anything that is suspicious; you can always email or call our friend even from another account and ask about it. If it is good it can wait a while.

59. Testing new products in small amounts

No matter how much you are in love with new product idea to sell, do not buy it in bulk, and test it in small amounts. See first that it sells and than buy more. Sell at least one first and than buy 5 or more, only than go to 10 peaces. Do not jump in new product without testing the water really well.

60. Your vacations for online business

On EBay and same on Amazon seller accounts there is a button to make a vacation mode, when you not selling. Use it wisely. Make sure it set and actually works, check if it works, log out and log in from another computer not logged in to your listings and see it they are still available for sale.

61. Dutch auctions

It is an auction different from regular auction when we start with smallest amount and over bid each other.
Dutch auction is an auction when everyone submits bids and who bid the highest number wins the auction.
Historically this method is not as successful and generally accepted as traditional English auction style. But it has its advantages and more appealing to seller than traditional auction, with more secrecy there is more chance that bidding sides will try over bid each other.

62. Niche marketing search

Very important in your business online is to find your niche what to sell, it depends if you know anything special about products you are about to sell. You would have to become some kind of expert on the subject to know all about what it made from, how it works, what is best, how long it last. You better love your niche because dealing with something day in and day out for a long time is boring and only if you like the niche you may stay fresh and follow new trends. See if you can add new to the existing product mix. What is your edge why you will be more successful than others on that subject?

63. Yard sales

Great place to find sales and unique items and invest in small amounts, you can go online right on the spot and search it worth and if it makes sense to buy it.

64. Antiques

EBay was made initially for antiques so it would be a perfect place to sell and buy those.

65. Selling arts

You can put invisible ink on back to make sure you are getting back your original in case you get a return

66. Seller jargon

In this section I will keep adding jargon words and terms that are popular with sellers, abbreviations. When you go to professional group message board you can see those words used left and right.

67. Storage lockers

Amazon has now storage lockers in major cities in the USA for people who stay at work during day time and do not want to receive private items in there office where everyone can see what they receive during day Amazon created places where people can receive stuff to the private lockers and that way avoid public eye of the competition.

68. **Vacation, travel, other people selling with you:** when you explain to your potential buyers that you have spare set of hands and extra mussels to work with you, that shows that you are serious business and capable to service even during holiday crunch time when everyone wants to receive gifts right on time for Christmas or other holiday and orders comes last day all at once.

69. Main computer has to be fast and free from virus

70. **Have a plan where would you print labels if your computer** will not work, and spell it out in your description, that gives some confidents to some potential buyers who want to be certain that you have capability to ship on time. If you have someone who understand your systems and has access to your product storage, spell it out, it also brings more trustworthy to your business.

71. **Holidays, many printers, many computers, trust reliability**. There is a button that you can press on amazon.com and on ebay.com that allows you

to put your account on vacation and go on vacation without totally delisting the products.

72. **Trade shows** Great place to find products for exclusive sales and great place to sell your products that you buy online and sell off line. You can look for ideas what to sell and see if there are actually many sales happen with other sellers before you jump in that product yourself.

73. **Successful examples**
Successful examples that I am planning to add to this book later on are my friend Oleg, my friend Alex and another Alex. I will get permissions from those people than I might be able to talk about there business. For now I would talk about my wife business online, I think she is a success. For someone who start without any knowledge in online business and to generate decent income for herself she is a success. In less than two years she graduated to a steady business with consistent profits.

74. **Virtual products kindle books, DVD, sounds, pictures**
Great place for EBay and Amazon to sell those products. Go for it, that is perfect place to advertise.

75. **Selling automobile**
I have a friend Eduard who is successful selling cars on EBay, in this section I would share some of the advice that he shared with me. Make car pictures in front of fancy houses, wash car before sale, perhaps have a pretty girl next to car all that is fair marketing tricks that increase probability of sale at higher price.

76. **Promotions on products**- it makes sense to offer promotions on products to create following, and to test how much more items you can sell in given period of time if you lower the price. You can play with that if you can afford but do not over due it. All is good in fair proportion.

77. **Product conversion rates** – you need to know how many of your ideas that you start to sell actually convert to profits, not every product that you start selling will sell great, as long as totally you make profits on all items together you are success. I try 10 items before I find one that actually starts to sell and product income. It takes time, marketing eye and experience to see what would sell at a profit. Research as such can be a product itself.

78. **Used products** – could be sold, no less than new products, ebay.com and amazon.com is perfect for that, just in description write all notes and describe the product in details. Different color, cuts, cracks, etc

79. **Referrals** – you can refer people to amazon.com and ebay.com and get 50 dollars for each actual new account that they will open, that is also money in your pocket.

Have your agreements with partners in writing. Who sells, who buys, who responsible for what. If you decide to separate how it will take place.

80. Unpaid disputes

To get your money in disputes and product, you need to have everything done by the rules. Show proof of shipment, call often to customer service to promote your case. Write notes to client. If client has wrong address, point it out. Each case is specific as time goes by I will keep adding specific cases that I encounter or seen with other sellers and solutions for resolution.

81. Borrow products from other sellers, borrow bubbles

You can borrow products from other sellers in your neighborhood in case you run out of product, and sold more than you have in stock. You can also find yourself in the situation when you run out of packaging materials and instead of buying in staples local store at retail prices, you can buy or borrow from your fellow sellers. And they can expect the same treatment for you. Share ideas, places to buy supply, suppliers some times if you trust a person. Share information if you getting money or other valuable information in return.

Opening new account

1. Need many feedback
2. Has to be open at least a year, otherwise easy to lose account
3. Learn drop ship
4. Work on increasing limits to sell more, always sell 90 to 100 of what your Limit let's you.
5. Need passport valid
6. Need address
7. Need local phone for the same country
8. Need SSN for USA or tax id
9. Need computer
10. Printer
11. Packaging
12. Supplier or products to sell
13. Ink for printer
14. Tape for packaging
15. Need to know where the post office.
16. Need camera, even phone camera is fine.
17. Need access to the internet.
18. Storage
19. Paper to print slips.
20. Envelops to pack products
21. Bubbles
22.

Reviews and feedback
Difference between feedback and reviews: feedback is given to you as seller and review you write on the product itself. So from review benefit all sellers of the product and feedback is specific only to the account that is doing sales.
There is a difference between reviews on amazon.com and ebay.com reviews on amazon.com can be publish for any product by any buyer as long as buyer have ever purchase an item on amazon.com from the same account. Amazon allows one review per product per buyer and reviews can be revised.

1. **Establishing feedback**- to start getting feedback and to have sales you need to start somewhere, on ebay.com there are two options that you have, you can start buying something very cheap and hope to get feedback for it and that is the way to gain feedback pretty easily and fast in terms of numbers, but that would not be quality feedback and people who understand what is going on, would be able to see that is buyer feedback with cheap items under one dollars for that reason done. You can fool some folks but experience ebayer you would not fool that easy. You also can visit local 99 cents store and start selling some cheap products below its cost, just to sell in bulk that would give you actual seller feedback and promote you as seller, will increase your seller limits and help you in terms of visibility.

2. **Feedback creation, growth**
Ask your buyers for feedback especially on amazon.com, many buyers do not know they can leave feedback on amazon.com. Submit requests for feedback. Send messages to buyers requesting feedback. Nurture your feedback, ask for it be polite, sell many items, do not expect to receive positive feedback from each buyer on Amazon, on Ebay you will probably receive nice feedback from every second buyer.
Give your feedback to them first that helps to break the ice and move in friendly direction.

3. **Leaving feedback**
Always leave feedback for folks, I do leave feedback almost immediately so people have good feeling about purchase they make. In the feedback you can say thank you, use your screen name, name product, all that helps to advertise to others who will be reading feedback you leave for others. Do not leave same feedback to everybody, it seems like machine. Have at least 4 different in template.

4. **Dealing with negative feedback**
On the Amazon account you can respond to feedback and on EBay you can respond as well. Try to explain to other customers what went wrong, explain if customer is unreasonable, explain your steps that you took to satisfy customer, see if other customers can see your side of story when they will visit your page.

5. **Prevent negative feedback**

Negative feedback is really bad for you. There are a few things that can allow you to save the situation. If you feel that you can get negative feedback from a customer try to prevent it by contacting customer and find common ground agreement. Offer refund, offer to send another free item, find out what is the problem, try to solve it, do everything possible to protect your feedback from negative, it really can affect your business in the negative direction, all the way to have you account permanently to get closed.
6.

7. **Review writing:** write as many reviews as possible try to receive reviews for the products that you sell, you can offer discounts for your products for the people who will write reviews for your products. I think that is a legal move on amazon.com. Establish yourself as powerful review writer with reputation that can help you in questionable discussions with Amazon and EBay staff. Build up your credibility. Try to do as many as possible video reviews, they are not that often yet on both sites and are quite valuable. Be specific, show the product, introduce yourself, speak clear, you can do reviews in a variety of languages if you speak more than one.

8. **Cost of reviews,** for each review from stranger you have to sell at least 100 books in order to get one unsolicited review. Ask people in off line world to give you reviews, ask friends, and as long at you not paying for reviews directly, amazon.com would not punish you. I find it is easy to ask for reviews from college students at campuses. Students have often nothing to do at campus and existing accounts. In order to leave a review each person can leave only one review per one product, but can modify his/her review any time. Accounts that have no purchases on amazon.com can not leave reviews, new account has to buy something, wait for it to deliver and than can leave feedbacks and reviews. Do not rush in leaving reviews before you receive product because amazon.com trace shipping and it would be suspicious to leave feedback and review same day as the order made. Cost of acquiring review should not exceed 50 dollars per basic reviews.

9. **Video review:**
Video reviews are very visual and great for promoting your product and yourself. Post as many as you can. Try to copy reviews on your youtube.com page so it will be easy to have all questions and answers about your products easily available to your potential buyers. How to open the package, to not damage what is inside. How to set up your product, how to clean your product, any possible questions that your buyers may have about product try to pre think and answer in advance. If you have been asked a question about your product, try to create a video with specific answer to it. That way you will create a library of answers and in the future you can point folks to the right answer.

There are verified reviews on amazon.com that are left by buyers who actually purchase item from you and then leave review and there are reviews just from people who want to talk about particular product or bought that product elsewhere and want to share their opinion with others in online community.
I would recommend copying good reviews for your products from amazon.com and adding to your website.
There are review written by professional review writers are to get those reviews are quite difficult and there are also reviews written by experts in the field that are also hard to get. Professionals are not so easy on positive and fluffy reviews. But those reviews work great. I find that number of reviews more important than reviews themselves because no one has time to read all reviews in detail. People look instantly which product has most reviews and go in. unless product is shit, they buy that one.

10. Promotional videos for your business
It is a good idea to make promotional videos about your business, brings you more legality, people can see your face, realize that actual life person or team of people is behind the operation. You can create questions and answers about products; you can explain your procedures. You can show how to use your products, you can discuss why your products better than competitions and share your side of story. Try not to offend others because that can cause retaliation, remember bad peace is better than good war. If it comes to closing your account on ebay.com and amazon.com it seams that they are less likely to close accounts to vocal people who go to media and are in the public eye. Both websites wants to be on your good side.

11. Ghostwriter
If your English is not so good or you can not write appealing descriptions or you sell very exclusive stuff and want your description to be perfect, you can hire a Ghostwriter some one who will write for you. Of course you would have to pay actual money but all the credit for the work can go to you and you get more Name for yourself and for your product. More respect from buyers can turn into more sales.

Selling techniques

1. Understanding buyers feedback and to whole not to sell

Read feedback of your buyers before shipping to them, if you see someone with no feedback or many negative feedback, perhaps it is not so wise to send them product, try to cancel order prior, do not look for troubles.

Negotiations and brand building

1. **Creating and keeping your brand** On each line of product that you start to sell if you do it yourself or it is generic, try to create a brand that would help you to differentiate from your competitors.

2. Brand name should be as short as possible, descriptive, and not reparative to other major brands. Has to be unique name, try to use your given name if you not ashamed, that brings credibility that you willing to put your name, like nobility. It is good to use your last name for the brand because it is proprietary and others would not be able to nock you out of your name. But if you choice generic name prepare for the fight, whoever invested more money in the promotion of the brand would have final ownership of the brand.

   3. **Making proper name for your seller accounts** You seller name is important for your perception by buyers. I would recommend to choice either your given name, that can give you unique name that no one else can compete with you for because it is given name, also it is noble to give to a business your last name, doctors have practice like Michael Smith MD for example or lawyers, that is a good practice. Also you can give female first name to business, that is also has good perception, you can use your spouse or if you are a lady, you can use perhaps your first name as seller. If you plan to sell one kind of products perhaps you can use name like King Cosmetics if you sell cosmetics, than choice names that are easy to spell so customers can return and buy more exactly from you rather than start search with all the sellers.

   4. **Brand:** create your own brand, control it, apply with amazon.com for the brand page and work your brand. That would distinct you from generic sellers and bring more trust to you. You would have more rights to protect your product line and link it to your website, your stores and your off line presence

5. Optimization, removing extra words, improves the language
Optimize your listings, less is better, people have no time to read to much of data, so whatever is irrelevant, try to be concise use only required data. If English is not your first language like in my case, I would recommend to ask someone to prove read your listings descriptions, some times you get some one do it for free, sometimes, you can pay actual money or pay with your product, that is also great way of moving more volume.

6. Your seller profile
Fill out your profile totally and once in a while update it, phone number, address, email, and website, everything they ask and volunteer more data. That gives your more credibility.

7. Low balling selling technique

Is a technique during negotiations when you offer to sell something at way lower price than it probably worth or others sell and when you get customer you make money on other services like shipments, packaging, require to buy other items where you make money or have really delayed shipping day like 90 days after you receive payments.
Not very much fair technique and you may end up with many negative feedbacks. Be careful.

8. Notes in seller account

If notes are necessary, put them in, that would be helpful to clarify a variety of situations. There are notes that can go to customer and notes that everyone can see. If you already faced one problem, try to prevent this problem in a future with other customers. Let them know what other already encounter in the past.

9. Trust between you and buyer

There are many ways to create trust between you and your buyer, give them a lot of information, show excellent fast customer service, be open to share address, phone. Show good feedback and many years of establish account.

10. Writing your business plan

At the end of the book I have attached a template for the business plan that you can fill out for yourself or for your potential investors, be honest with yourself, look at your business from many angles.

11. Your partners for online business

Some partners can duplicate your services some partners can supplement you, some partners can invest money and some partners can share ideas, it does not have to be equal shares between partners. You can have partners who contributed account to sell from, you can have partners who contributed product to sell, you can have partners when one partner works certain hours and service account and than second partner service account. Like in case of two nurses or doctors who go in shifts and during their shift can not answer email and do shipping, in that case it would beneficial to have partners to service account if you have fast selling product that requires immediate respond.

12. Legal advices for online sale

I am not a lawyer so I can not give legal advice for money. My best advice is to see someone you trust local, in case your question is very much specific to EBay or Amazon account you can always find a lawyer specializing in that kind of business, this group of professionals who give legal advice about online businesses grows daily. For many questions that you might have you can find answers online, just type in Google and you will be surprise how many similar situations to your other people encounter and shared online.

13. Customer mailing list

Keep a list of customer addresses, names and email and if you have phone numbers, that can lead to repeat purchases directly from you, referrals to friends, and selling to them other similar products directly or via websites.

14. Negotiation on price

In some cultures, not to negotiate is rude so some folks would be offended if you buy from them without negotiation, they would feel that you think too little of them personally that they sell so cheap, by negotiating with them you so respect that you are interested in product. In that case negotiate, be polite, explain how your price come up, explain product specifications and benefits, I would say try to get all potential sales. Product can be sitting in your storage way longer than you anticipate.

15. Counter offer

When you see a price some where it does not mean that is final price, you can counter offer. And quite often you will get a little bit of discount 5 to 10 percent discount on large item or many small items is still money. So do not be surprise when you are asked for discount when someone send you counter offer. I tent to accept most of counter offers that get especially if they are reasonable. I am not going to sell at my cost or bellow, but I would go for the offer from real customer just to move more product at the given day. Just be careful, not to sell the house to strangers bellow your cost. You can write to buyer an explanation why the price is so and so. Because competition charge more, or because your product is unique in some way, or for other reasons. Once person understand how your price structured, person can accept original price. Also that gives you an opportunity to explain benefits of your product directly to potential buyer, if they see value in your product, you may sell more than one item and get very satisfy customer.

16. Fob free on board

Term that could be used by your international suppliers in whole sale. Still make them to spell it out and describe what they mean by that, sometimes even simple words could mean other things in other peoples ears.

17. Selling a kit versus separate products

Great tactics is to create new products is buying mixing existing products in the set. That allows you to be special and if you mix proper products in the set you can sell more products and sell even at the premium some times.

18. Post sale sequence of events-
   a. Check if item is paid in case ebay.com
   b. Check if you have any messages from that buyer, sometimes they write to cancel order after placing it and not know how to cancel order other than message, that would save you on all following steps

    c. Locate product, because if you can not find the product you would need to return funds and save on label and other steps.

    d. Print package slip, that would tell you cost of shipping, sometimes you want to cancel order if shipping cost is more than what you plan for.

    e. Print label for postage

    f. Locate package and bubbles

    g. Leave feedback for buyer, thankful explaining that you ready to ship

    h. Package product, prepare bags to carry to post office

    i. Take to post office

    j. Watch out for returns,

    k. Watch

19.

Customer Service

1. Paying for the VIP client service

Customer service: check your messages often, connect your ebay.com and amazon.com service to your mobile smart phone, so you will be connected

Fqa

Seller stories and examples from real life

1. Sveta drop ship buyer for Dubai
2. asking to remove negative feedback with gifts
3. what do you need to open account

Negotiations styles

- American (Yale, Harvard, NYC, South)
Direct, straight to the point, fast, not wasting time, require quick results.
Could be won by taking time, prolonging conversation, could be accepted as distributive or apple pie.

- Asian
Asians try to avoid direct confrontation, would say yes to the face or avoid permanent answer and then find excuse or without explanation will look for better deal somewhere else with someone who understand their culture better.

- Eastern Europe
Eastern European is a collective culture bargain so they tend to ask for advice from friend or family member. Also if a few sales people confirm that product is good they may buy, but if just one person would tell those about product, their individualism would not let them buy just on personal instincts versus western civilizations where most of the decisions made personally by the person at the chair.

- Japanese
Japanese like to pay attention to details, love poker face, and consider emotions affect badly fair deal. Also like to go for the whole deal rather than share responsibility.

- Canadian (very pleased and smile, testing partners for little favors, try to consider the other side feeling carefully) looking for pleasant relationship after negotiations, very collaborative style

- European
Difficult to read, friendly outside but have no personal attachments, won usually by being patient, cordials, be more trustful, less chance of being left alone in the deal.

- Brazil (abrupt, tend to be late at in time to show who is boss, substantial emphasis on power, personal friendship means a lot.

Age difference in negotiations

- Child
Children tend to pay attention to things that are immediate, bright, loud, very little consideration to others feeling. When negotiate with child try to use power and respect as more experienced person. Draw more examples. Bring emotions in negotiation, tend to ask for help from other adults in case they can not get the deal they want

To be successful in negotiations you need to lead a child, paint a picture with your words, be exciting.

- Adult

Adults pay attention who to who has the power in negotiation, look to over power the opponent.
To be successful in negotiations you need to have power or show respect to their power,
Watch their personal space.

- Senior

Seniors like to take their time, not to be rushed, look for long term results. Pay attention to trust issue.
To be successful in negotiations you need to build trust, listen for real buying signals, take your time, patience.

Segregate bigger issue and details

Some negotiations parties would consider all the issues on the list, you need to consider bigger issues as with more weight rather than smaller details. That way you may give up in many little things and win a bigger deal where it matters.

- What is more important to comment on that moment issue and yield argument on small deal and win big deal

Appeal to nobility

Many people want to feel noble so by asking for higher ground you bring to negotiations to the level of honor and nobility that way people may forget some past disagreement in a desire for future collaboration. It feels good. Very powerful appeal

- Ask for good will, if person likes you he/she may give you a bit of free space waiting for reciprocity on your side
- Perceive the other side as kind and they will act kind even if they are evil

People think of them self as good even if they are very bad, so by considering and showing respect even with evil person you may evoke in him/her a good spirit and get some good reciprocity and collaboration

- Appeal to the best in other party

That way you give a person a chance to forget their evil side and act only as noble persona, since others do not see that in them, I try to very respectfully address in full name without any familiarity that way they feel more honor and less desire to cheat me out of fair deal, even if other side consider that as weak approach I would stick with strategy that way negotiation can keep going on and I have always an opportunity to walk away, but I give them no reason to walk away

- Reason to healthy thinking

Every person thinks of him/herself as rational thinker, by trying to reason like the

Godfather in Mario Puzzo book you get a chance to see every angle of the deal.

Eye contact

Eye contact very important, it gives a person a chance to look you in the eye. Some nationals like Russians pay a lot of attention to human eye. Do not blink to much, appear calm. Look directly into person eyes but not too long that could be considered intimidation. Especially if man looks in the woman eyes she may consider him interested in something more than negotiation on the table and respond irrational to deal at stake. Cordially smile when you look at someone eyes, that way you remove the threat even if that is your intention, it just intensify your desire to get to the bottom of things to do the best possible deal.

- Body language (adjust body to the best position)

Crossing legs is a bad sign in many nations, consider of hiding something, also the same for crossing hands on the chest also a symbol of closed mind
Hands on a table visible with ladoni open, collaborative movements.
Touching hair or scratching is a bad sign for not saying the truth.
Playing with watch or ring removes attention from topic and take attention, although when presentation is length and other party attention is disoriented it is helpful to flash bright object like watch or ring and knock on table that bring them back to what is at the table.
Sit straight, do not slouch, do not lay back, that is the sign of to relax and disrespect. Too much leaning forward is a sign of to much want a deal, invasion on others space.

- Remove noise from your pose

Everything like stripe shirt can take others attention from the topic and make them think about stripes distance from one to the other rather than listen your message. Color shirt can be interpreted as not fully respected meeting. White shirt is always the best. Even blue shirt can mean routine meeting, and for the best meeting of your life, you would wear white shirt like for your wedding day. Button your top button, that means mean business and no slack, straight tie mean straight spine and knowledge of the discipline and honor. Do not wear anything that can take attention from what is at the desk.

- Acknowledge does not mean to agree

Sometimes the other party wants you to make believe their side of the issue and would pressure you to see their views in their eyes. The best is to acknowledge their view and respectfully acknowledge that is not the same as agreeing, otherwise they would feel comfortable that you accept their view now and later on back down from earlier position. You may look like someone swaying both ways and not reliable partner. Be firm but that does not mean that you should lose attention of the other side.

Selective perception
When you talk others may only listen to what they want to hear, rather than full story, let's say good and bad sides of your product/ proposal. Try to accent points

that the other side may miss so later it would not sound like you did not mention those points and you would be called liar or cheat. There are more important and less important parts of your presentation, try to get other party best attention spin when you talk about important aspects more.

- Reciprocity

People are reciprocal creatures. It is nice to take advantage of that feature. Many stores gives free samples or do something for free for you in hope that you in return buy their products and cover eventually expenses for the initial free gesture. Take and give is very deep in human emotions even many animals have that instinct like the dog when its bring you toy. Little gifts and favors matter.

- Social prove (testimonials)

Many businesses are sold applying testimonials that is something that works in society with deal collective roots. There are different ways to show respect and power of your presentation/product, recognitions and awards in the office is one of the ways to show social prove that what you do is attested by someone or better professional as proper solution. Doctors, lawyers have their diplomas in the office as well as licenses on the walls as prove that society attest that they know what they do.

- Scarcity (the less person available, the more influential he/she is)

People have a weak spot for conspiracy theories. One theory is that the fewer people available the more that person is important and desirable to deal with. That is because wealthy people or people at power are busy and less available to the public so less busy person may want to appear busy and not available so others perceive him/her as busy, someone knowing what hi/she is doing.
Not always true, usually you can accomplish more by being open to conversation, more flexible than the other guy. That way you may hear about business opportunity that person that appear to be busy.
The good use of scarcity is when the other party does not respect your time and effort and think that you can work for free, has lack of respect for your desires. In that context to show that you are busy and would not waist your time for nothing is a good thing and may show other side that they over archive zone of possible deal and now they have to start to cooperate. It is the time when you can change them a bit more to get even, do not go in that direction. Stay fair as if they been fair to you from the beginning that would earn you respect and trust.

- **Visibility**

Being visible is very important in sales, it makes you at the top of the news, Facebook, twitter, and other social media accomplish that in some way in addition to tradition advertisement like newspapers, TV, and other media.
Being approachable help you to be the first choice of business.

Salami tactic

Comes from ancient army tactics by Alexander Macedon's, it means divide and concur. Is a way to take control of the meeting? Appeal as you have the authority to tell them what to do and you know how it deals lay down.
Break problem to smaller peaces.

- **Divide and concur**
Cherry picking
Is the tactic when you can choice clients to deal with from large pile and you deal only with the wealthier customers or only perceptive customers to your ideas, or you pick only the best clients from plenty of opportunities or start with those where you get the most chances to make a sale?
A good strategy if you do have limited time and many options but eventually lucks systematic approach on the down side.

- **Choice best customers to deal with at the moment**
Value your time, try to deal with the most important issue at hand and than move to less important, priorities if you allowed. For example a sales person in the store is not allowed to service customers with large orders first and than everyone else who wants to ask a question.

- Value lays with fair strategy for all (public companies versus private)
Parable Orange concept
- One need cover
- The other needs juice
- Planting an orange tree or orange orchard
The idea behind orange is that if you get to place an orange on a table and you and I have to negotiate who gets it or bigger peace of the orange we can negotiate weather it should be 50/50 shares or I get 70 and you get 30 percent but at the end it would be tough for each one of us to get the whole thing and even if we share 50/50 still neither one accomplish his/her goal. But what if we move from distributive behavior and start to talk about integration. We may discover that I want the orange cover to make candy and you want orange juice, that way I can have all the cover and accomplish 100% of my goal and you can have all the juice and get your desire. What if we keep talking and realize that we may have a field where to plant seeds from the orange that way we can have a tree that will annually give you all the juice and I can get covers. What if we can expand the conversation and we can plant orange orchard, that way we can sell many oranges and provide for our families. That is an idea of expanding a pie to bigger picture partially by repositioning so neither one needs to compromise his/her goals. Not always easy to get it done but a great way to discover other issues that could be added to the issue on the table.

- **Accept only creative outcomes**

By that I mean that solutions that are fresh and new and created together have tendency to stick longer and be distinct and create more business. Try to think in negotiations out of the box, re invent yourself, your product, you proposition every time you get a chance. You have the right to be smarter tomorrow than you are today.

- **Understand cultures, especially your own.**

Before going to the negotiation territories try to understand you first. Who you are in negotiations, what mistakes you make. Knowledge of how you negotiate would give you an idea what to do to take best advantage of that and know your weaknesses and weak spot. You can work on improvement of your style and adjust according with whom you negotiate. You may want to consider explaining your negotiation style to the other side, explaining your culture, perhaps the other side will reciprocity and share there view on the issue. That way you can look for common ground.

- **Don't just adjust to cultural differences, exploit them**.

Take advantages of the cultural differences. Learn the other side at the table, may be they would like to learn your ways.

- Gather intelligence and reconnoiter the terrain.

The more you know about your partner at the table the more you can use that information later on at the negotiation to advance your view.

- Design the information flow and process of meetings.

Try to have an exchange of ideas, find time for you to speak and time for the other side to speak, that way you know that you have a partner on the other side, otherwise you may lose their attention.

- Invest in personal relationships.

When it is personal it is always better rather than just a suite, get to know the other side, share some good information about yourself that would make you more human in the eyes of the other side, more likable

-

- Persuade with questions. Seek information and understanding.

If you find out why the other side is saying that they are saying, you would be able to address it appropriately, also you may see a solid reasoning in their agenda. It is never late to adopt a better vision if that is the case, not all good ideas in the world have to come from you, incorporate others solid thoughts in your presentation. That may help you to understand your position better.

- Make no concessions until the end.

Is a good strategy, as long as you know where the end is? May be you need to look at the beginning. You know beginning is a better word than end. Beginning starts things and end finish. Sales and negotiations are usually about beginning of the new chapter rather than closure.

- Use techniques of creativity

- Continue creativity after negotiations.

From wikipedia
- Establish common goals of what this "collaboration" would create. A more workable deal? Some common long term goals? A closer partnership?
- Establish the rules of engagement. The purpose of the exercise is to resolve differences in creative ways that work better for both parties. All ideas are possibilities, and research shows that combining ideas from different cultures can result in better outcomes than those from a single culture.
- Trust is key, and difficult to establish in many cultures. Certain techniques might speed that process a little. Being offsite, for example. Establishing physical proximity that unconsciously signals intimacy.
- Add diversity (gender, culture, extroverts, different work specialties, experts, outsiders) to the group. Indeed, the diversity associated with international teams and alliances is the real goldmine of creativity in negotiations.
- Use storytelling. This both helps establish who you are and what point of view you are bringing to this collaboration.
- Work in small groups. Add physical movement. Tell the participants to relax, play, sing, have fun, and silence is ok.
- Work holistically and using visuals. If, for example, there are three sticking points where neither side is happy, agree to work on those points by spending a short time – 10 minutes – on each point where both sides offer "crazy" suggestions. Use techniques of improvisation. Neither side should be offended by the crazy ideas. No one should criticize. Explain that by exploring crazy ideas that better ideas are often generated.
- Sleep on it. This enables the unconscious to work on the problems, and gives negotiators time to collect opinions before meeting again the next day. Other kinds of breaks, coffee, etc. are also helpful. The overnight part is particularly important. Anthropologist and consumer expert Clotaire Rapaille suggests that the transitions between wakefulness and sleep allow new kinds of thinking "…calming their brainwaves, getting them to that tranquil point just before sleep"
- Doing this process over several sessions allows both sides to feel that progress is being made, and actually generates better and more polished ideas that both sides can invest in.
- It is the process of creating something together, rather than the specific proposals, which creates bonding around a shared task and establishes new ways of working together. Each side feels honored and all can feel that something is being accomplished.

Ask questions or not to ask questions?

It depends sometimes it is time to listen and absorb without interaction and misdirection, see where that can lead, it can open some information that you have not thought to ask.

Asking questions can help you to lead conversation in the direction that you want to follow.

• Too many questions
Too many questions can be perceived and obnoxious and never ending and you may miss real buying signals when it was time to sign and you miss because you ask questions when it was time to sign the deal.

• Not enough questions
If you move to close the deal too fast you may miss important peace of information. It has to be the right mix

Use palm of the hand from back or front

Sub processes
Perception

Levels of conflict
• Conflict in yourself (ideas, thoughts, emotions) negotiate with yourself
One of the things that you can do before the sales meeting you can negotiate with yourself. First it would be practice for yourself, second of all you would know how far you can go in what direction, you would know your position.

Your ideas can be not shared by other side. Is that necessary as long as you getting what you want from them in the deal?

Your emotions, if you are passion about the product or presentation that you make that helps to sell, but it also can cloud your judgment and prevent you from seeing some truth in the other side position. You thoughts could be also incomplete on the subject and other side may bring a better or distinct view on the subject, try to learn those thoughts it may help you at the next negotiation table with someone else or at the next round of negotiations with that partner.

• Conflict within different groups
There are different groups at the negotiation table, there is a party that is represented, it could be also its lawyers or union members who represent their interest. It could be younger generation like son or daughter representing a senior at the negotiation table with nursing home. And the interested of the party often a bit different from the interest of the party. Perhaps son who represent father at the nursing home negotiations does not have father best interest at heart, just want father out of the house. Or perhaps union leadership just wants to collect their salary and show that they do something in reality very little done

for the union members. Or lawyer want to collect his fee either way the case would go so, lawyer does his/her best not always the best thing for the case. We will examine different ways how to deal with the party interest.

Third party introduction
- Liabilities
- Mediation

Mediation is the situation when someone represent both sides of the party and wants concord. Judge sometimes performs that function but also try to obey the law, not only interests of the parties and interest of the public. For example in child custody cases battles judge mostly look for the benefit of the society that child be not a burden to tax payer and than for the interest of the child than for the interest of the mother and than for the benefit of the father if any left. Usually in those negotiations, there is a lot at stake and each party, like lawyers, court and parents have a bit different priorities.

Remedies
- **Getting mad**

Sometimes works and calms the opposite side. But sometimes it can get them scared or reserve from further communications and the door for future negotiations can be closed.
There are times when getting mad means that the side reaches the end of the zone of possible agreement and that is what causes the emotion as the symbol. No more.

- **Getting even**

Is a bad tactics that leaves bad taste in mouth because there is always reciprocity in getting even from the other side as well and that leads to end of the collaboration, hurt the bottom line of both sides?

- **Tensions and de escalations**

Tensions could be caused by not understanding other side position or time frame deadline or pressure to sign the deal, all that usually drives away from the deal It escalates the situation to unmanageable that is the situation when someone can be shot or killed.

- **Ultimatum**

Is a tactic when an opponent threaten to do something unless, that is my lowest price. If you refuse that proposal I walk away or go to your competition. It is very difficult to hold face in case the other side calls your bluff. Ultimatum can work very well with someone who has no other choice or not prepared for other offers or feel threaten by your ultimatum otherwise it is a very bad practice, because it rarely has repeated business. Only sadomasochistic person would deal with someone who thread with ultimatum more than once. In some cultures that is necessary tactic because otherwise the opponent feels that they can bargain further and further and only when he/she hears ultimatum that they feel that is end of the bargaining discussion.

- **Being difficult**

Is a way to negotiate, is a good strategy when you deal with someone who may be threaten and really dependant on you. Otherwise that can tarnish reputation and that strategy close doors to future negotiations. No one like difficult customers and next time you will experience hire price to cover the humiliation of dealing with difficult person or black refusal to deal with. Usually people with being difficult strategy end up at the end with worth deal than pleasant people because sales person sells them the first thing they willing to buy and wants them on the way out of his/her face. They do not get all the facts, but minimum information in order to get rid of them. The more you talk with someone who play being difficult card the less desire to share information with such a person, so they end up with worth deal. People who place being difficult card, do not a benefit of a doubt that next sale could be beneficial, so it becomes just one time transaction. Usually those people complaint later on any way, no mater how great deal they get, so what is the point to give them best deal. Better to charge them premium, considering that in the future there is more effort to be wasted for complaints, litigation. Those people end up with the most plain vanilla product that does not require a lot of interaction with exchange of information and as result not the best not creative deal.
The best tactic to deal with being difficult person is to listen, write down their requests. Present your offer on paper. Try to explain that by being difficult customer/client/ partner they may not have partner at the table at all.

Differences

- Self – Efficacy

When a salesperson always right he/she feels that what ever challenge in front of him/her they can concur. That brings too much of the confidence and a real partner at the table can feel that demands of such a person are unreasonable and deal could be lost. Only people with low confidence can bite such a behavior. And that is substantial chunk of population

- Self – Monitoring
- Omnibus approach
- Interpersonal trust

Coalitions

It is easier to negotiate if a group of negotiators organize together like a union or party or group.
I participate in group of fishermen and hunters to get better price for the expenses shared on trips.
Also groups of buyers for the apartments from the developer gets a better deal than individual buyers of the apartments.

- Multi party negotiations
- Pre negotiations

Very important, that prepares you to know your "best alternative to not negotiate" prepares all the ideals on the table, consider how the deal can be expanded,

Integrative negotiation

In my vision that is the best negotiation strategy that creates long term relationship and end up with more business and more good relationships than any other strategy

- **Flow of information**

A substantial part of the integrative negotiations is and exchange of information that way parties get to know what each party needs to know about the other to present its case and see the case of the other party in others eyes.

- **Commonalities emphasis**

Paying attention to commonalities helps parties to build some kind of bond that in the future can hold negotiations together. Russians like to deal with Russians, African American wants to deal with African American, and man like to deal with man on sensitive issues as their reproductive health for example. Woman wants to talk to woman on the issues of the heart and that commonalities factor plays well in negotiations.

Try to discover if there is type of food that you and your party likes, consider if there are common places that you visit or originally from and the other party from. If there is common interest. You are married with kids and the other party also married with kids.

- Joint solutions

Look for the solutions that both parties contribute

- Define problem
- Generate alternative solutions
- Common goal or objective
- Validity of the position
- History of relationship

Distributive bargain

- Settlement point
- Cost to terminate negotiation

- Other party expectations, cost to terminate
- Tactics
- Opening offer, stance, initial concessions
- Role of concessions
- Final offer

Sub processes
- Anchoring
- Winner curse
- Overconfidence
- Small number law
- Serf services biases
- Other cognitions
- Reactive devaluation,

Good words
- Reason
Justice
Ethics
- End result
- Rule ethics
- Social Contract
- Personalistic ethics

Bad words
- Sales
- Positions

Gende
Sales tactics overcome
- How to beat low ball tactic
- How to beat kind practice
- Misdirection
- High voice
- Silence

Avoid response when?
- Address it later
- When to avoid

- When to forget (Corleone)
- Dismiss
- Power adjustment

When to be balanced and when not to be balanced
- Anger
- Loud
- Fair
- What is better being positive or neutral?

Why compromise is bad?
Conflict management
- Contend – domination
- Yielding – accommodation or obliging
- Inaction
- Problem solving- collaborate, integrate
- Compromise

Heuristics
- Perception of loss or gain

Time and duration of negotiations
- Last minute concessions
- Conditions before negotiations
- Breaking negotiations to many small negotiations
- Discussing whole picture versus detail analysis

Separate issues from people
- Positions are not good
- Discuss ideas
- Proposals
- Different views on same issue

How would you characterize yourself and your counterpart
- Reputation
- Reliability
- Experience
- Education
- Comfort level

Aspirations prior to negotiations

- Low
- High
- In level

Process of dispute

- Fight
- Low key
- Breaking frames

High emotions

Israel – Palestinian negotiations

- Religion
- Passion
- History
- Rightfulness

Chinese Negotiation style

- Social linkage
- Harmony
- Roles
- Reciprocal obligations
- Saving face

Goals and wishes are different

- Link our goals and other party goals
- Measure goals
- Break tangible versus intangible
- Choice, chance, interdependence, imperfect information

Unilateral concessions – good or bad?

- Israel
- Other viewers
- Later, next state
- Guilt

Minimum goal max goal

- Interest, likeliness, chance for future collaboration
- Max goal – check today and contract for the rest of life
- Step by step
- First impression

- Leaving to desire for more
- Every day like last day, over performance

Trust and openness
- Know your needs and motivations
- Know other needs and motivations
- Predictability (good or bad)
- Aggressiveness (bluff, upper hand)
- Remedies
- Self dignity

Phases
- Initial
- Problem solving
- Resolution
- After and before prepare
  > Prepare and resolve everything prior to negotiation
- Than be open minded during negotiations
- Be creative
- Do not forget your bottom line
- Try to get more than what you planned

Consulting with others
- Ground rules
- Location of negotiation (yours, mine, neutral, hotels, restaurant) territory
- When to introduce other parties (prior, during, after?)

Setting targets
- Optimism (not to be upset if fail)
- Realist (leaving money on table, no extra satisfaction of getting more than plan)
- Pessimism (weak position)

Trades off prepare
- What to give up
- List of what to gain

- Order in what issues are introduced
- Size of trade offs

Bargaining mix
- Single deal always could be expanded to multiple deals
- (train yourself for future deals similar)
- Discover other things to deal about
- Try new strategy, practice, experiment
- Perfection of one time shot

Remove the other party resistance point
How to research other party
- Internet
- Friends
- Competition

- Pattern of concession making
- Commitment
- Power of first move

Establish commitment
- Finality
- Consequences
- Specific
- Public announcement

How to abandon a committed position
- Given what I learn today
- Let matter die in silence
- Re state commitment in more general terms
- For the good of public or company good leave position
1.

Equality between buyer and seller
- American
- Canadian
- Italian
- French
- Russian
- Japanese
- Chinese

- Brazil

- Argentina
- Israel
- Arabic
- Iran
- British
- Korean

Intellect affection on negotiation style
- Aggressiveness
- Truth
- Size of the pie
- Preparation
- Disclose emotions and goals
- Ask questions

Use of time for your advantage
- Americans in patient
- If someone in a rush
- If someone has extra time, how to use that to your advantage,
- Give what the other side wants in abundance
  Discuss the whole deal at once or segregate to small peaces
- Big picture
- Paining attention to particular details

Prisoner dilemma
- Two suspects are arrested by the police. The police have insufficient evidence for a conviction, and, having separated both prisoners, visit each of them to offer the same deal. If one testifies (defects from the other) for the prosecution against the other and the other remains silent (cooperates with the other), the betrayer goes free and the silent accomplice receives the full 10-year sentence. If both remain silent, both prisoners are sentenced to only six months in jail for a minor charge. If each betrays the other, each receives a five-year sentence. Each prisoner must choose to betray the other or to remain silent. Each one is assured that the other would not know about the betrayal before the end of the investigation. How should the prisoners act?

Create value versus create relationship

Sample of the business plan template

I.   Executive Summary.

II.   Situation Analysis.
   A. Industry analysis.
     1. Market.
        a. Size, scope, and share of the market; sales history of producers and their market shares.
        b. Market potential and major trends in supply and demand of this and related products.
        c. Distribution channels.
        d. Selling policies and practices.
        e. Advertising and promotion.
     2. Industry attractiveness.
       a. Market factors.
          1) Size.
          2) Growth.
          3) Ciclicity.
          4) Seasonality.
          5) Stage in life cycle.
       b. Industry factors.
          1) Capacity.
          2) New product entry prospects.
          3) Threat of substitutes.
          4) Power of suppliers.
          5) Power of buyers.
          6) Rivalry.
       c. Environmental factors.
          1) Social.
          2) Political.
          3) Demographic.
          4) Technological.
          5) Regulatory.
   B. Sales analysis.
     1. Market area performance versus company average.
     2. Trends of sales, costs, and profits, by products.
     3. Performance of distributions, end-users, key customers.
     4. Past versus current results by area, product, channel, and so on.
   C. Competitor and company analysis.
     1. Behavior.
         a. Product features.
         b. Objectives.
         c. Strategies.
         d. Marketing mix.
         e. Profits.

        f.   Value chain.
    2. Resources.
        a. Ability to conceive and design new products.
        b. Ability to produce and manufacture.
        c. Ability to market.
        d. Ability to finance.
        e. Ability to manage.
        f.   Will to succeed in this business.
 D. Customer analysis.
    1. Who are the customers?
    2. What do they buy?
    3. Where do they buy?
    4. When do the buy?
    5. How do they choose?
    6. Why do they select a particular product?
    7. How do they respond to marketing programs?
    8. Will they buy again? (loyalty)
    9. Long-term value of customers.
   10. Segmentation.
 E. Planning assumptions and forecasts.
    1. Market potential.
    2. Projections, predictions, and forecasts.
III.   Objectives.
 A. Corporate objectives.
 B. Divisional objectives.
 C. Overall marketing objectives.
    1. Sales volume and profit (sales, share, and so on).
    2. Market acceptance (brand equity; customer acquisition, retention, expansion, deletion).
 D. Program objectives.
    1. Pricing.
    2. Advertising/promotion.
    3. Sales/distribution.
    4. Product.
    5. Service.
IV.   Marketing Strategy. How the objectives will be achieved.
 A. Customer targets.
 B. Competitor targets.
 C. Core strategy.
 D. Strategic alternatives considered.
V.   Marketing Programs.
 A. Product development.
 B. Advertising/communication.
 C. Pricing/promotion.
 D. Distribution.
 E. Sales.

      F. Direct marketing and customer management.
      G. Internet.
      H. Services.
      I. Partnerships/alliances.
      J. Market research.
VI.   Financial Documents.
      A. Budgets.
      B. Pro forma statements.
VII.   Monitors and Controls. Specific research information to be used:
      A. Secondary data.
           1. Sales reports.
           2. Orders.
           3. Informal sources.
      B. Primary data.
           1. Sales records (Nielsen, IRI).
           2. Specialized consulting firms.
           3. Customer panel.
VIII. Contingency Plans and other Miscellaneous Documents.
      A. Contingency plans.
      B. Alternatives strategies considered.
Miscellaneous.

Homework for the EBay Amazon students

1. make pictures for listing
2. do listing
3. come up with name of brand
4. Write feedback on eBay
5. Write feedback on Amazon
6. write a review on Amazon
7. find products for sale and write why they would sell and make profit
8. list your supplies
9. list your post office schedule
10. picture policies
11. listing policies
12. security policies
13. study and read few books on EBay and Amazon
14. find seller friends
15. go on seller eBay community boards
16. research your dashboard
17. study shipping rates
18. read few chapters from my book
19. write your seller policy
20. write you shipping policy
21.

Sponsors

www.AlexGurman.com swimwear bikini with glow in the dark beans, to order you can go on amazon.com and ebay.com Alexander@AlexGurman.com or 917 825 8225 (we look for musicians to add music to our videos, new models and additional photographers at different world locations, product placement ads, other creative promotion)

www.BargeFishing.com korablik for fishing trout, most productive on the river with the current, swims with a current and against it. You can order directly via email Alexander@AlexGurman.com or 917 825 8225 or buy at our stores on Amazon.com and EBay.com

www.FishingBaitGlue.com fishing bait glue for carp and other fish, glues life bait to hooks as well as glues dry bait to hook like sunflower seeds, you can order directly via email Alexander@AlexGurman.com or 917 825 8225 or buy at our stores on Amazon.com and EBay.com

www.SvitlanaHolovko.com dog and cat photography and videography and ebay.com and amazon.com seller, trading assistant, you can learn how to sell products on EBay and on Amazon or become vendor supplier for our stores. Contact at HolovkoSvitlana@gmail.com or 646 515 0786

www.VetVittles.com sausages for dogs and pet herbal products, you can buy on our website, phone 888-807-4588 or email vet@vitvittles.com

www.FullPetServices.com veterinarian clinic and grooming place in Brooklyn, NY, USA admin@fullpetservices.com or 718 891 2370

Russian American Dogs and Cat Club

ModelMayhem 3139021 photographer Svitlana Holovko provides photography and videography for your events like weddings as well as referrals for professional models for glamour and product photography. Contact at HolovkoSvitlana@gmail.com or 646 515 0786

ModelMayhem 3151176 photographer Alexander Gurman Alexander@AlexGurman.com or 917 825 8225
Books by Alexander Gurman on Fishing and Hunting and about selling on Ebay.com and Amazon.com are selling on Amazon.com and EBay.com, books cover variety of topics such as where to fish, how to fish, what tackle to use and how to assemble this tackle. Alexander@AlexGurman.com or 917 825 8225
www.TheGroomingBook.com grooming books.

Your advertisement could be hear also.

Conclusion and references

www.amazon.com
www.ebay.com
www.alibaba.com
www.aliexpress.com
www.overstock.com
www.etsy.com
www.barnesandnoble.com
www.google.com

There are many resources where you can get more in information. Try things, products, and techniques. Ask questions. Call customer support.

Printed in the USA
CPSIA information can be obtained
at www.ICGtesting.com
LVHW082239110824
787984LV00031B/885

9 781304 194787

MEDITERRANEAN & BULGARIAN cuisine

12 Easy Traditional Favorites

Ronesa Aveela

Copyright © 2016 Bendideia Publishing

November 2016

ISBN-13: 978-1540389855
ISBN10: 1540389855

All rights reserved.

All rights reserved. Except for use in any review, the reproduction or utilization of this work in whole or in part in any form by any electronic, mechanical, or other means, now known or hereafter invented, including xerography, photocopying and recording, or in any information storage or retrieval system, is forbidden without the written permission of the publisher: Bendideia Publishing, www.ronesaaveela.com.

This is a work of non-fiction. Tomato (AdobeStock_66196512.jpeg), olives (AdobeStock_102622050.jpeg), and plate (AdobeStock_116864295.jpeg) images are used in accordance with Adobe Stock photo Standard license agreement. https://stock.adobe.com/license-terms. All other photographs are © Nelinda.

Cover Design and interior art © Nelinda, www.nelinda.com

Editing by Bendideia Publishing.

Contents

Bulgarian Cuisine 1

    Banitsa 3

    Katmi 5

    Patatnik 7

    Sarmi 9

    Rhodopean Klin 11

    Zucchini with Yogurt 13

    Thracian Guvetch 15

    Tikvenik 17

    Rhodope Baked Beans 19

    Easy Baklava 21

    Koledna Pitka 23

    Lazy Koledna Pitka 25

About the Author 27

Ronesa's Books 27

Reviews 28

Bulgarian Cuisine

These recipes were originally published in *Light Love Rituals: Bulgarian Myths, Legends, and Folklore*. I'm offering them to you as a separate book so you can enjoy the taste of dishes Bulgarians have enjoyed for centuries—whether they are original to the region or shared by neighbors along the Mediterranean Sea. No finer tradition exists than making Bulgarian cuisine, which is as rich as the soul of the people. The meals, like the colors woven into the nation's rugs, represent the hospitality and rich spirituality of its people. From the mystical Rhodope Mountains, the birthplace of Orpheus, to the Thracian Valley, known for its roses, whether the dishes are light or hearty, they will always be savory. Some of the recipes have a modern twist to make them easier and more interesting.

Bulgaria's varied and colorful cuisine has been greatly impacted by ancient history, diverse traditions, and customs, as well as being influenced by the exquisite spiciness of the East and the elegance of European cooking. If you wonder why these dishes have a unique, unforgettable taste, it's due to the method in which food is cooked and the type of cookware used. In some regions, people still use "ancient" cooking equipment like embers and earthen ovens (*podnitza*). More commonly, though, they use colorful clay pots (*guvetch*) and copper or earthenware frying pans (*sach*). Food cooked in a clay pot doesn't require using unhealthy fat and needs only a small amount of liquid, so the food retains its nutrients and vitamins. Meats in particular remain tender.

Among the traditional Bulgarian dishes are beans cooked in a clay pot, meatless *sarmi* wrapped in grape or cabbage leaves, and stuffed dried peppers with rice or crushed beans. But the queen of all dishes is *banitsa* (cheese pie). Made everywhere in Bulgaria, it's prepared differently in each region, which contributes to its specific taste.

Another national specialty is *katmi*, similar to pancakes or crêpes, but a little thicker than the latter. The main ingredients vary, and may include milk, yogurt, eggs, yeast, and tap or sparkling water. It's best to cook them on a *sach* over an open fire, so the wood contributes to their unique flavor.

The variety and combination of spices used on the food also make the taste unforgettable. Some of the main ones are dill, mint, savory, and parsley. One of my favorite spices is *sharena sol*; its ingredients are summer savory, paprika, and sea salt. You can find this spice at the table of almost every Bulgarian home. Magical spices add not only to the taste, but to the aroma as they cook.

Bulgarian yogurt, which comes in more than one hundred varieties, is another important ingredient in many traditional Bulgarian foods. What could be better on a hot summer day than *tarator*? This cold soup, made from yogurt, water, finely grated cucumbers, garlic, and dill, is not only refreshing, but also healthy.

Don't forget a good wine to bring out the real taste of your gourmet meal. Similar to the different traditions and rituals, each region in Bulgaria has its own local wines. It's no wonder, since Bulgarians have been producing wine since the time of the Thracians. Wine lovers have a plethora of quality wines to choose from.

Or perhaps you prefer *rakiya*, a brandy made from plums or grapes with your meal. Or even *gyul*, rose brandy.

Whatever your choice, *Nazdrave*, "Cheers, to your health!" I hope you enjoy the traditional recipes that follow. As a bonus, I've added a modern twist to some to help you discover the diversity of the Bulgarian kitchen.

Banitsa

1 lb (500 g) feta cheese	4 eggs
1 1/2 cups yogurt	1 lb (500 g) filo dough
1/2 cup sunflower oil	Egg yolk

Banitsa is the queen of Bulgarian cuisine. The most popular version uses a filling of white cheese (feta cheese) and eggs. If you travel to Bulgaria, you can try variations of this dish with different fillings: pumpkin and sugar (*tikvenik*), cabbage (*zelnik pie*), onion, spinach, and rice (*klin*) (from the Rhodope Mountains), meat, and others. Another type of *banitsa* uses milk, eggs, and vanilla, and is served as a dessert. The popular dessert *baklava* is also a type of sweet *banitsa*.

STEPS:
Preheat oven to 375°F (190°C).

Make Filling
- Crumble the feta cheese and mix it with the yogurt.
- Add the oil and mix well.
- Stir in the eggs and make sure the mixture is consistent.

Prepare Dough
- Flatten the package of filo dough sheets and using a brush or a spoon, sprinkle a small amount of oil or butter onto the top sheet and smear it around.
- Add a spoonful of the filling and spread it evenly over the entire sheet.
- Roll the top two sheets into a log and arrange the log onto the outer edge of a round baking pan that has been greased with butter or oil.
- Continue making more logs and place them in the pan in the shape of a spiral until you have used all the filling and the pan is filled.
- Mix one yolk with a few drops of water and coat the *banitsa* with it.

Final Steps: Bake the *banitsa* for about 35 min. or until the crust is golden. After baking, cut the *banitsa* into pieces. You can eat it hot or cold. It is usually served with yogurt and can be part of your breakfast or lunch.

An easy modern *Banitsa* variation: If you want to make this an appetizer to impress people, use small wonton wrappers. Push a wonton wrapper into the bottom of each of the eight sprayed cups in a muffin tin. Spoon the egg-and-feta-cheese mixture evenly into the wonton wrappers. Bake for 18 - 20 minutes until golden brown. Let cool 5 minutes before removing from the muffin tin. For a richer taste, add spinach or ham to the feta cheese mixture. In the end, you will have a variety of appetizers.

My Notes and Tips

Visit **www.ronesaaveela.com** to explore recipes from Maria's Kitchen. Learn about different Bulgarian and Mediterranean dishes and try the taste of Emona and the Balkans.

www.ronesaaveela.com

Katmi

Package of yeast	4 cups (1 liter) milk
1/2 cup warm water	3 eggs
1/2 teaspoon salt	4 cups (0.5 kg) all purpose flour
1 teaspoon sugar	1 egg yolk
	Butter or cooking spray

Katmi are similar to pancakes, but they are cooked on a special shallow clay or copper pan. In most places in Bulgaria, they are prepared without eggs.

STEPS:
Cook on a burner on top of the stove.

Prepare Batter
➢ Mix a package of yeast with warm water.
➢ Add salt and sugar.
➢ Mix well and let the yeast dissolve.
➢ Pour milk into another bowl and add the eggs.
➢ Slightly beat the eggs with a spoon until they are a liquid consistency.
➢ Stir in the yeast until it is mixed throughout the egg batter.
➢ Add flour a little at a time and stir in the mixture until it thickens.
➢ Set the batter aside at room temperature or in the oven to allow it time to rise. Bubbles will appear on the surface when it is ready.

Cook Batter
➢ Preheat the frying pan on medium heat, or use a flat crêpe pan or cast iron pan.
➢ Separate an egg yolk into a small bowl, and slightly beat it with a spoon.
➢ Coat the pan with butter or olive oil cooking spray.
➢ Pour the stirred yolk over it.
➢ Pour a heaping spoonful of the *katmi* batter onto the pan. Move slowly to cover the bottom of the pan equally. It will form a shape similar to a crêpe. Turn the *katmi* over
➢ with a spatula when the top bubbles or shows holes (only a few seconds). Cook until the other side turns brown.

Toppings: When the *katmi* are ready, pour melted butter over them. Then spread on jam or honey, and sprinkle nuts on top. You can roll them up like crêpes, or layer them like a cake, with a filling of your choice in between the layers. Serve them warm, or cold like an appetizer.

My Notes and Tips

Visit **www.ronesaaveela.com** to explore recipes from Maria's Kitchen. Learn about different Bulgarian and Mediterranean dishes and try the taste of Emona and the Balkans.

www.ronesaaveela.com

Patatnik

2 lbs (1 kg) potatoes
1 egg
7 oz (200 g) feta cheese
Parsley or mint
Pinch of salt
Black pepper based on your taste

2 Tablespoons melted butter
Onion
Green peppers (optional)
Mushrooms (optional)
Ham (optional)
1 Tablespoon cooking oil

Patatnik is a slow-cooked potato dish from the Rhodope Mountains region. It is a simple meal made with grated potatoes, onions, salt, and *gyosum* mint. Other non-traditional ingredients you can use are white cheese (*sirene*) or eggs, in addition to savory and peppers. I sometimes add mushrooms and bits of ham to make it a complete meal. This version uses feta cheese, but you can use any type you like: provolone, white American, etc. Serve warm and enjoy a taste of the Balkans.

STEPS:

Prepare Ingredients
➢ Peel and grate the raw potatoes. Set them aside in a spaghetti drainer to remove the potato juice.
➢ Grate the feta cheese in a small bowl.
➢ Take a handful of the grated potatoes and with both hands squeeze them to remove extra juice, and then put them in another bowl.
➢ Repeat the above step until you have all the potatoes in the bowl.
➢ Stir in the grated feta and the egg.
➢ Add the parsley (or mint), salt, black pepper, and melted butter.
➢ Stir until well mixed.
➢ Chop and add the onion.
➢ Chop and add the green peppers, mushrooms, and ham (optional).

Final Steps: Pour cooking oil in a large, deep skillet (nonstick or cast-iron is best). Turn heat to low. When it's hot, pour in a thin layer of the batter. Shake the pan occasionally, and adjust the heat so the batter doesn't burn. Cook until the bottom is nicely browned, at least 15 minutes. Turn the *patanik* over by sliding it out onto a plate then covering it with another large plate. Invert the plates and slide the *patatnik* back into the pan. Add more oil as necessary.
Cook until it becomes golden on the other side. You can also bake it in the oven.
Preheat to 375°F (190°C). Generously butter an oven-proof dish. Pour the potato mixture into it and bake about 30 - 40 minutes, or until the potatoes are tender. Sprinkle with parsley and grated cheese. Serve warm.

My Notes and Tips

Visit **www.ronesaaveela.com** to explore recipes from Maria's Kitchen. Learn about different Bulgarian and Mediterranean dishes and try the taste of Emona and the Balkans.

Sarmi

1 (16 oz) jar grape leaves
2 - 3 carrots
2 onions
1 cup vegetable oil
1 cup of rice
1/2 lb (500 g) ground beef

1/2 cup water
Pinch of sea salt
Paprika, dill, parsley
1 teaspoon chopped garlic
1 stick of butter
2 - 3 cups of water

Traditionally in Bulgaria, *sarmi*, or stuffed grape leaves, are served with yogurt (seasoned with garlic and salt), or you can cover them with *béchamel* (a white sauce made from butter, flour, and milk).

STEPS:
Preheat oven to 350˚F (190˚C). Cover the bottom of a pot with small pieces of cabbage or grape leaves. It's better to use a clay pot with a cover, and cook the *sarmi* on low heat.

Prepare Ingredients
➢ Drain the grape leaves and carefully pull them apart.
➢ Finely chop carrots and onions.
➢ Heat a frying pan on low heat and add the vegetable oil.
➢ Add the carrots, onions, rice, and ground beef to the heated oil and stir.
➢ Pour in 1/2 cup of water.
➢ Add salt, paprika, dill, parsley, and garlic to taste, and stir.
➢ Cover and boil on low heat until the rice is swollen, but not fully cooked.

Fill the Grape Leaves
➢ Place the grape leaves on a flat surface, and add a spoonful of the mixture.
➢ Wrap the leaves into a log.

Fill Clay Pot
➢ Place the *sarmi* on top of the pieces of grape leaves in the clay pot.
➢ Cut butter into small pieces, add to the pot, and sprinkle with dill and parsley.
➢ Slowly add 2 - 3 cups of water (enough to cover the *sarmi*).
➢ Hold down the *sarmi* with a plate so they don't unwrap.

Final Step: Cover the pot and cook for 30 - 35 minutes.

Variations: You can use fresh cabbage leaves or sauerkraut instead of grape leaves. If you want to add more flavor, add 2 - 3 crushed walnuts to the stuffing. Cover the *sarmi* with chicken broth rather than water. If you don't want to cover the *sarmi* with a plate, you can simmer them at 200˚F (95˚C) for about an hour.

My Notes and Tips

*Visit **www.ronesaaveela.com** to explore recipes from Maria's Kitchen. Learn about different Bulgarian and Mediterranean dishes and try the taste of Emona and the Balkans.*

Rhodopean Klin

1 lb (500 g) feta cheese
1 cup boiled white rice
1 lb (500 g) fresh or frozen spinach
1/2 cup sunflower oil

4 eggs
1 lb (500 g) filo dough
Egg yolk

The Rhodope Mountain region, homeland of Orpheus, is one of the most beautiful places in Bulgaria. Its people treat you with hospitality. *Klin* is a specialty *banitsa* from this region. It is deliciously warming and easy to make, proof that simple things are often the best. The filling is made with rice and spinach. Alternate ingredients are kale or other greens according to your mood, creativity, and the season.

STEPS:
Preheat oven to 375°F (190°C).

Prepare Filling
➢ Crumble the feta cheese and mix it with the rice and spinach.
➢ Add the oil and mix well.
➢ Stir in the eggs and make sure the mixture is consistent.

Prepare *Klin*
➢ Flatten the filo dough, removing 8 sheets to cover the bottom of a shallow baking pan. The pastry should overlap the edges.
➢ Gently smear the top sheet with oil or butter.
➢ Spread the filling evenly over the sheets using a spoon.
➢ Take another 8 sheets and cover the filling and fold over the top.
➢ Gently sprinkle with oil or butter.
➢ Mix 1 egg yolk with a few drops of water and coat the *klin*.

Final Steps: Bake for 35 min. or until it looks golden. For best results, bake for 20 minutes, take the pan out of the oven and turn it upside down on a plate. Flip the entire *klin* over so that it lands in the pan, the opposite side up. Cook for another 20 minutes. After baking, cut the *klin* into pieces.

Variation - Versatile *Klin* wontons: To make an appetizer, use small wonton wrappers. This quick recipe makes a great crunchy afternoon snack or a meal when paired with a bowl of soup on a cold winter day. Position the wonton wrapper with one point toward you. Place 2 spoonfuls of filling in the center of the wrapper. Fold the bottom corner over the filling. Fold the sides toward the center over the filling. Roll toward the remaining point (shape of a log). Moisten the top corner with water or egg yolk and press to seal. Repeat with remaining wrappers and filling. Place on baking sheets coated with oil. Lightly coat wontons with oil or butter and yolk. Bake at 375°F (190°C) for 15 - 20 minutes or until golden brown, turning once.

My Notes and Tips

Visit **www.ronesaaveela.com** to explore recipes from Maria's Kitchen. Learn about different Bulgarian and Mediterranean dishes and try the taste of Emona and the Balkans.

www.ronesaaveela.com

Zucchini with Yogurt

1/2 cup plain yogurt
2 teaspoons chopped fresh dill
1 small clove garlic, grated
1/2 teaspoon lemon juice

Salt
Freshly ground black pepper
1 lb (500 g) zucchini
1 teaspoon olive oil

Bulgaria produces more than 100 varieties of yogurt. Not only is it eaten plain, it is used when cooking or preparing many dishes. It is no wonder, since yogurt was invented by the Thracians, a fact about which Bulgarians are proud. From a cold drink during the summer to a hot lunch, yogurt is certain to be an ingredient.

STEPS:
Cook under broiler.

Prepare Dill Mixture
➤ In a small bowl, whisk together the yogurt, dill, garlic, and lemon juice. If necessary add a few drops of water to make the mixture of pourable consistency.
➤ Season to taste with salt and a pinch of black pepper.
➤ Set aside.

Prepare Zucchini
➤ Trim the ends off the zucchini and cut it into thin slices or strips (circles or long strips).
➤ Toss with olive oil, salt, and pepper.
➤ Place the zucchini in an oven-proof skillet or pan and broil, flipping occasionally, about 10 minutes until slightly charred and tender, but not mushy.

Final Steps: Remove from broiler. Serve zucchini warm or chilled, covered or dipped in the yogurt-dill sauce.

Alternatives: If you want a richer taste, coat the zucchini with flour. Place the pieces (circles or strips) into a frying pan with about a half inch of heated oil. Fry the zucchini pieces until they are golden brown and crispy. In the summer, you can use a grill instead.

Other Yogurt Ideas
Tarator - Bulgarian Cold Cucumber Soup.
Airan - a drink made of yogurt, cold water, and salt.

For more great ideas, check Maria's Kitchen page on MysticalEmona.com.

My Notes and Tips

Visit **www.ronesaaveela.com** to explore recipes from Maria's Kitchen. Learn about different Bulgarian and Mediterranean dishes and try the taste of Emona and the Balkans.

Thracian Guvetch

Savory and fresh parsley
1 onion
1/2 lb mushrooms
2 tomatoes
1/2 lb feta cheese
Cooking oil

Chili powder
Black pepper (or hot peppers)
1/2 lb smoked or precooked
   chorizo sausage
1/4 cup grated cheese
2 eggs

One of the tastiest Bulgarian cuisines is a meal prepared in a clay pot (*guvetch*). Bulgaria has as many variations of the *guvetch* as it does regions. Throughout the centuries, people adapted the recipe by using available ingredients. Every time my mother made this dish, it was different and more delicious than the last time. Cooking it in the *guvetch* was the reason. The pot itself is quite colorful, a piece of art. Bulgarian ceramics are unique and the designs are full of imagination. A classic type of Bulgarian pottery is called *Troyan*. If you don't have a *guvetch*, you can use any type of clay cooking pot. The idea is to experiment and discover different flavors to enhance your food.

STEPS:
Preheat oven to 420˚F (215˚C).

Prepare the Ingredients
➢ Chop the parsley, onion, mushrooms, and tomatoes.
➢ Slice the feta cheese into tiles.

Fill the *Guvetch*
➢ Pour a little cooking oil into the pot and place some onion on top.
➢ Arrange lines of feta cheese, then mushrooms, then tomatoes, and the remaining onion.
➢ Sprinkle with parsley and savory.
➢ Add chili powder and black pepper or whole hot peppers if you prefer to cook with them.
➢ Arrange the sausage on top. If you can't find chorizo, you can use any kind of precooked or cured smoked sausage.
➢ Cover the pot and place it in the oven.
➢ Bake for 15 - 20 minutes.
➢ Remove the lid and sprinkle with grated cheese.
➢ Crack both eggs on top and bake for another 10 - 15 minutes.

Final Steps: Remove from the oven and sprinkle with fresh parsley. Combine with a glass of red wine and enjoy the taste of Bulgaria and the Balkans.

My Notes and Tips

Visit **www.ronesaaveela.com** to explore recipes from Maria's Kitchen. Learn about different Bulgarian and Mediterranean dishes and try the taste of Emona and the Balkans.

Tikvenik

1 1/2 lbs (680 g) pumpkin or
  butternut squash
1 cup sugar (or brown sugar)
1 teaspoon ground cinnamon
2 oz (55 g) chopped walnuts

Honey
1/2 lb butter (2 sticks), melted (optional)
1 lb (500 g) filo dough
2 - 3 Tablespoons powdered sugar
  (for sprinkling on top)

Tikvenik is a sweet pumpkin *banitsa* made mostly in the fall and winter months. It is a common food served on *Koleda* and *Budni vecher*.

STEPS:
Preheat oven to 350°F (190°C).

Make Filling
➤ Mix together the sugar, cinnamon, and walnuts in a small bowl.
➤ Cut the pumpkin or squash into large chunks and grate it.
➤ Add the walnut mixture to the grated pumpkin/squash.
➤ Add a few drops of honey.
➤ Pour the melted butter over the pumpkin/squash mixture.

Prepare Dough
➤ Open the package of filo dough and spread it out.
➤ Cut it horizontally and vertically into 4 equal pieces.
➤ Remove 2 sheets from one pile and place the filo with a point facing you.
➤ Sprinkle vegetable oil or melted butter over it (not more than a teaspoon).
➤ Spread 2 - 3 Tablespoons of the pumpkin/squash mixture evenly over the filo (so it slightly covers the surface).
➤ Sprinkle some of the leftover sugar on top of that.
➤ Fold the corner facing you over the filling, then fold the two sides over that.
➤ Roll the filo toward the remaining point so it is shaped like a log.
➤ Place the log on a greased baking dish, with the open end down.
➤ Repeat the process until all the filling is used.
➤ Sprinkle vegetable oil over the top, coating the filo so it doesn't become dry.

Final Steps: Bake for about 20 - 30 min. until the filo is crispy and golden on top. Remove from the pan immediately after baking and let it cool. Sprinkle lightly with powdered sugar.

Variation: If you don't like pumpkin or squash, use apples instead. Make sure to drain some of the juice from the apples, but not all of it. Before you bake it, sprinkle grated apple and nuts over each piece to add a little bit of a twist.

My Notes and Tips

Visit **www.ronesaaveela.com** *to explore recipes from Maria's Kitchen. Learn about different Bulgarian and Mediterranean dishes and try the taste of Emona and the Balkans.*

Rhodope Baked Beans

14 oz (400 g) of white kidney beans
2 onions
1 carrot
Celery
3 - 4 Tablespoons vegetable oil
3 - 4 Tablespoons flour

Red pepper to taste
2 tomatoes, grated
Savory, mint
Smoked sausages
1 package pizza dough

This is a variation of a famous recipe for *Smilian* beans, named after a town in the Rhodope Mountains. There is even a Bean Museum there. This hearty meal of beans topped with fresh baked bread is perfect for a long, cold winter day.

STEPS:
Preheat oven to 375°F (190°C) after beans are cooked.

Prepare Beans
➤ Put the beans in a pot of water and leave to soak for about 12 hours.
➤ Drain the water and add fresh water.
➤ Bring it to a complete boil, then lower the heat to medium.
➤ Slice one onion, a carrot, and some celery.
➤ Add them to the boiling beans.
➤ When the beans are soft, turn the heat low and let them simmer.

Prepare Bean Bullion
➤ Put 3 - 4 spoonfuls of vegetable oil into a frying pan, and turn on low heat.
➤ Chop the second onion and put it into the heated oil.
➤ Cook until it gets soft and a little clear.
➤ Sprinkle it with flour and red pepper.
➤ Stir occasionally.
➤ Once the flour and onions are cooked, add 1 scoop of beans.
➤ Mash and fry them for a short time only, so the flour doesn't burn.
➤ Grate the tomatoes and mix them until they form a smooth paste.
➤ Pour the tomato paste onto the beans in the frying pan and let it boil until the beans are cooked.

Final Steps: After the beans are cooked, preheat the oven and fill 4 clay French onion soup bowls (or any clay pot) with beans and add a little of the bean bullion until they are half full. Add savory and mint. Cut up some sausages and add them. Fill the clay pot up to the cover line. If you have time, make biscuit dough from scratch. Otherwise, use ready-to-bake pizza dough and make 4 "caps" to cover each clay pot. Leave the pots until the dough rises. Bake about 35 minutes until the dough is cooked. Remove the pots and let them cool off a little.

My Notes and Tips

*Visit **www.ronesaaveela.com** to explore recipes from Maria's Kitchen. Learn about different Bulgarian and Mediterranean dishes and try the taste of Emona and the Balkans.*

Easy Baklava

1 package puff pastry shells (6 shells)
1/2 teaspoon ground cinnamon
1/2 cup chopped mixed nuts
1/2 cup butter, melted

1/2 cup white sugar
1/2 cup water
1 teaspoon honey
1/2 teaspoon vanilla extract
1/2 teaspoon grated lemon zest

Baklava is a well-known dessert served not only on *Koleda* and *Survaki,* but also throughout the year. The dessert was listed in a thirteenth century Turkish cookbook. The following is a modern recipe I invented that saves time and hassle.

STEPS:
Preheat oven to 385°F (200°C).

Prepare Shells
➢ Butter a round shallow baking dish.
➢ Toss together cinnamon and nuts in a small bowl.
➢ Break open a package of pastry puffs along the pre-scored lines to separate the shells. Take them out of the freezer at least 4 - 5 hours prior to baking.
➢ Place the puffs onto the baking sheet with their tops up.
➢ Brush them generously with melted butter.
➢ Sprinkle 2 - 3 Tablespoons of the nut mixture on top.
➢ Bake for 20 minutes, until puffs rise and are crisp and golden.

Prepare Syrup
➢ While the puffs are baking, combine the sugar and water in a small saucepan over medium heat and bring to a boil.
➢ Stir in the honey, vanilla, and lemon zest.
➢ Reduce the heat and simmer for 30 minutes.

Final Steps: Remove the puffs from the oven and let them cool for 15 - 20 minutes. Spoon the syrup over them. Let them cool completely before serving. Store uncovered. The best way to bring out the flavor of *baklava* is to let it cool for about 24 hours. When it is dry, make an additional syrup mixture and spoon it over the top of the puffs.

Variation: Use puff pastry sheets. Spread the nut mixture onto a sheet, patting it down with your hands. Sprinkle melted butter on top. Start rolling the log from the filled edge until you have a firm even log. Using a sharp or serrated knife, cut the log into 1/2 inch slices. Place them on a waxed-paper lined tray. Preheat oven to 385°F (200°C). Bake for about 15 - 20 minutes or until golden brown. Prepare the syrup and the rest of the recipe as described above.

www.ronesaaveela.com

21

My Notes and Tips

*Visit **www.ronesaaveela.com** to explore recipes from Maria's Kitchen. Learn about different Bulgarian and Mediterranean dishes and try the taste of Emona and the Balkans.*

Koledna Pitka

1 package yeast	4 cups (1 kg) flour
1 teaspoon sugar	4 cups (1 liter) water
1 cup (1/4 liter) lukewarm water	Walnuts
1 teaspoon salt	Dried fruit

Koledna Pitka, or fortune bread, is the most important part of the meal on *Budni vecher*. It is a round loaf of bread with a coin and possibly fortunes inside. The top is decorated with dough, either religious symbols or ones representing the family occupation (birds, cross, letters, plough, sheep, and so on). In some regions, it is decorated with dry fruit and walnuts.

STEPS:
Preheat oven to 375°F (190°C) after the dough has risen.

Prepare Starter Dough
- ➤ Add the yeast and sugar to a large mixing bowl.
- ➤ Pour the lukewarm water over the yeast and sugar to dissolve them.
- ➤ When dissolved, stir the mixture with a spoon.
- ➤ Slowly add half a cup of flour, stirring it until well mixed.
- ➤ Let the yeast mixture rise.

Knead the Dough
- ➤ Sift the remaining flour together with the salt.
- ➤ Pour the flour into a large round pan and form a "well" in the middle.
- ➤ When the starter dough rises to twice its original size, put it into the well.
- ➤ Stir it with a spoon at first to mix with the flour, then afterwards knead it with floured hands.
- ➤ Slowly add 4 cups of lukewarm water, kneading the dough into the flour as you do this until all the flour has been mixed into the dough.
- ➤ Put the dough on a greased tray and cover with a cloth.
- ➤ Let it rise in a warm place until it is double in size.

Final Steps: While waiting for the dough to rise, write fortunes on a few small pieces of paper. I usually do one for each member in the house or dinner party. When done, roll each fortune in foil. Wrap a coin in foil as well. When the dough has risen, knead it once again and spread it carefully in a baking pan. Distribute the fortunes equally throughout the dough. Decorate the dough with walnuts and dried fruit. Put the pan into a preheated oven to bake.

   At the dinner table, break the bread and give each person a piece. Make sure to leave the first piece on a plate. This is the fortune for the entire household. Enjoy your fresh bread and have a great and prosperous new year.

My Notes and Tips

*Visit **www.ronesaaveela.com** to explore recipes from Maria's Kitchen. Learn about different Bulgarian and Mediterranean dishes and try the taste of Emona and the Balkans.*

Lazy Koledna Pitka

2 loaves frozen dough
1 egg
1/2 cup feta cheese crumbs

Since we are all busy and time is the only thing we are short off nowadays, the following variation to *Koledna Pitka* is my version of the bread in a modern and easy-to-do style.

STEPS:
Preheat oven to 375˚F (190˚C).

Prepare First Loaf
➢ Leave the frozen dough at room temperature until it gets soft.
➢ Spread oil in a baking pan to prevent the dough from sticking to the sides.
➢ Place one loaf in the pan. I like to use a round baking pan, not a shallow one, so the dough doesn't overflow the edge when it rises.
➢ With kitchen scissors, cut the loaf into small thin strips.

Add Fortunes
➢ Write fortunes on a few small pieces of paper. I usually do one for each member in the house or dinner party. When done, roll each fortune in foil. Wrap a coin in foil as well.
➢ Insert the coin and fortunes into the dough.

Prepare Second Loaf
➢ Mix the egg and feta cheese crumbs together and spread evenly over the top of the loaf.
➢ Cut the second loaf into small pieces and place them over the first one, covering the feta-cheese mixture.
➢ Sprinkle with feta cheese or use grated cheese, the same as what is used for pizza.
➢ Cover the pan and let the dough rise at room temperature or near the warming oven until it has doubled in size.
➢ Bake for 30 - 35 minutes.
➢ Let it cool near the oven for another 30 minutes.

Voila! Here is the lazy Bulgarian's *pitka* baked with love!

My Notes and Tips

*Visit **www.ronesaaveela.com** to explore recipes from Maria's Kitchen. Learn about different Bulgarian and Mediterranean dishes and try the taste of Emona and the Balkans.*

About the Author

Ronesa Aveela is "the creative power of two." Two authors that is. The main force behind the work, the creative genius, was born in Bulgaria and moved to the US in the 1990s. She grew up with stories of wild Samodivi, Kikimora, the dragons Zmey and Lamia, Baba Yaga, and much more. She's a freelance artist and writer. She likes writing mystery romance inspired by legends and tales. In her free time, she paints. Her artistic interests include the female figure, Greek and Thracian mythology, folklore tales, and the natural world interpreted through her eyes. She is married and has two children.

Her writing partner was born and raised in the New England area. She has a background in writing and editing, as well as having a love of all things from different cultures. She's learned so much about Bulgarian culture, folklore, and rituals, and writes to share that knowledge with others.

Connect with Us!

Social Media: Website/Blog | Newsletter | Facebook | Twitter | Instagram | Pinterest | Goodreads | Bookbub | LinkedIn | YouTube |

Promo products: Redbubble

Ronesa's Books

Fiction
Mystical Emona: Soul's Journey
The Unborn Hero of Dragon Village
Zmeykovo (Bulgarian version of *The Unborn Hero of Dragon Village*)
La profezia del Villaggio del Drago (Italian version of *The Unborn Hero of Dragon Village*)

Nonfiction
Light Love Rituals: Bulgarian Myths, Legends, and Folklore
A Study of Household Spirits of Eastern Europe
A Study of Rusalki – Slavic Mermaids of Eastern Europe
A Study of Vodyanoy – Water Spirit of Eastern Europe
    (free gift when you sign up for Ronesa's newsletter at https://dl.bookfunnel.com/1rq3ku0fa9)
Skitnikut – usmivki I sulzi: Rasmisleniata na edin bulgarski emigrant (Bulgarian version of *The Wanderer*)
The Wanderer – A Tear and a Smile: Reflections of an Immigrant (available March 2020)

Children's short stories, activity & coloring books
Baba Treasure Chest series
The Christmas Thief
The Miracle Stork
Born From the Ashes
Mermaid's Gift
Baba Treasure Chest: A Collection of Modern Bulgarian Tales (contains all four short stories)

Coloring Books
Mermaids Around the World
More Mermaids Around the World
Little Zoi

Cookbook
Mediterranean & Bulgarian Cuisine: 12 Easy Traditional Favorites

Reviews

PLEASE HELP AUTHORS BY LEAVING A REVIEW!

We hope you've enjoyed this book. We would appreciate your gift of a review. Good or bad, we'd love to hear your honest thoughts.

Made in the USA
Monee, IL
19 April 2021

65224324R10021